C000071664

Drawn b

Adventures in Patagonia

Meg Robinson

An author in search of characters.

Copyright © 2009 Meg Robinson

All rights reserved.

ISBN: 1-4392-5724-8

ISBN-13: 9781439257241

Visit www.booksurge.com to order additional copies.

Drawn by a Star

An Irish artist's trials and triumphs on a personal quest to Patagonia

Meg Robinson

In memory and respect for my Irish,
Dutch and Jewish ancestors.

For my sons

and my beautiful grandchildren.
Also for my treasured daughters in law.

For my Irish family.

And for Wither, Tatiana and Maurito
my new 'family' in Peru.

It is strange to be here. The mystery never leaves you alone. Behind your image, below your words, above your thoughts, the silence of another world waits. A world lives within you. No-one else can bring you news of this inner world.

John O'Donohue, Anam Cara

Your job as author is to find the story within the story.

Catherine Ann Jones

Table of Contents

Part 2: The Road to Andres

Foreword

by
Chris Stewart
Author of 'Driving Over Lemons'

IN GENERAL, travel writers don't give you the whole story: you know full well that they are keeping the real stuff back. Meg tells it like it is, though, and by means of telling all she adds an extra lustre to those moments of joy and illumination that, for the traveller, make travelling worthwhile, that put your feet back on the road time after time. It's a deceptively simple trick, but I think, having read this delightful book, that I've figured it out. It's this: Meg has the gift of writing straight from the heart.

"PATAGONIA IS NOT A PRECISE REGION ON THE MAP. IT IS A VAST VAGUE
TERRITORY THAT ENCOMPASSES 900,000 SQUARE KILOMETRES OF CHILE
AND ARGENTINA." (BRUCE CHATWIN)

Introduction

"Patagonia is the farthest place to which man walked from his place of origin. It is therefore a symbol of his restlessness. From its discovery it had the effect on the imagination something like the Moon, but, in my opinion, more powerful." (Bruce Chatwin)

I'M A FRIENDLY, adventurous, exiled Irish artist who loves wilderness, a fairly new grandmother and I'm about to embark on a three-fold mission to South America. My assignment will take me back to the wilds of Patagonia where last year I left a large part of my heart.

Firstly, I'm searching for a story to make into a film. Secondly, I'm hunting for a new place to call home. And thirdly, there's a mysterious, remote, legendary pioneer village set between two vast ice fields that I'm drawn to explore. But plans have a way of changing when intuition becomes our internal compass, which is another way of saying—anything can happen when we're drawn by our star.

IT ALL STARTS on the first day of 2007 when I bump into Wes, a young Canadian sculptor friend, in our local market town in Andalucía.

We collide beside the lottery kiosk. It's a bright, sunny, wintry morning. The sky is cobalt blue, cloudless. The sort of January morning that makes expats' hearts sing.

"What's your new year's resolution?" he asks. "A big exhibition? Have a book made of some of your images?"

"No," I say slowly, not knowing what to say next. "Actually—I want to get back to scriptwriting. I'm going to write a screen play. I'm going to write a film."

I allow this statement to settle and fill the space between us. There follows an excited silence and an exchange of wide-eyed looks. I'm extremely surprised to hear these small words sail out of my mouth, and I spend the rest of the day grinning because I **know** in my bones I'm going to do this. In seconds I'm sparkling and glowing inside with excitement. I explain to my friend that I wrote two plays for television, a stage play which was performed at the Edinburgh Festival and a film script in the 1980s. I've done my apprenticeship in scriptwriting, I tell him. He smiles and nods.

We part and I enter a new chapter of my life right beside the lottery kiosk. The alchemy begins.

So, my first task is to find a story. I feel certain I'll find it in Patagonia.

I'M NOT SURE what kind of a story I'm looking for. Maybe it'll be a powerful modern legend, or an enchanting contemporary fairy tale with a twist, or a brave emigration story or an exile story? At the moment I've no idea. But I know I'll know when I've found it. I need a theme, a plot, and characters with challenges to overcome. My main character has to be somebody people can identify with, somebody people will love. Somebody who has a relentless, unfulfilled need. A person with an unusual life challenge and a disempowering personality flaw which makes achieving his or her goal unlikely, but in the end inspirational. My previous plays were based on my own life challenges in my thirties and forties. This time it's going to be other people's challenges, set in Patagonia, backed up by life experience. After all, I'm a grandmother artist/writer now. Many years have slid into the drawings and diaries of my past and many life lessons have been learned. If I don't find this story now—who knows?—maybe I won't have another chance to paint the bigger picture I see.

My second project is to find a home for next winter. Winters in southern Spain aren't cold, but Chile has captured my heart and I want to spend more time there, every year. I'd love a simple wooden house beside a turquoise lake in a small village in southern Patagonia. I love living in my mountain village in dry Andalucía, but I miss water. I need more water in my life. I'm also looking for 'my South American tribe'. I want to find where I belong in Patagonia, where I feel at home. Where I fit in.

And thirdly, equally important, there's the wildly mysterious, extremely remote pioneer village Calleta Tortel to discover. For the last year, I've been drawn to Tortel like a tiny drawing pin to a massive magnet. This attraction is something to do with the difficulty in reaching the village; few visitors get there. And something to do with an extremely strong inner hunch I cannot argue with or dismiss. It's been whispering to me constantly over the past year that in this one-of-its-kind village, an important person or a vital lesson—or both—is waiting for me.

CALLETA TORTEL (Tortel Cove) has been inaccessible except by boat until 2004 when Pinochet's beautiful and legendary unpaved highway, the Carretera Austral, branched inland to reach a point above the village. The village lies at the top of an inlet, set between the massive northern and southern ice fields of Patagonia. There are no roads or pavements in Tortel, only gangplanks, timber walkways and weathered ladders connecting the two hundred or so primitive wooden houses. For over five decades, Tortel and its surrounding area have attracted fearless wilderness explorers and exciting scientific expeditions from around the world. It also attracted Father Giuseppe, a brave and kind Italian Catholic missionary, who in 1955 returned to the village with a boat-load of domestic animals: a cow, a pig or a sheep for each starving family.

My plan is to travel the two thousand five hundred kilometres from Santiago to Tortel first by plane, then by boat, then by local bus. Most of the journey, I hope, will be by local ferry. Maybe everything will come together in Tortel, a fascinating legend on which to base the film; a small wooden house to rent beside a turquoise fjord and a new tribe of kindred spirits.

TWO DAYS AFTER RETURNING from this 'mission' to Patagonia, I invite a friend to supper. She brings two strangers; a clown-turned-plumber and an Irish actress. We sit around the kitchen table, talking about art. When the ice cream is almost finished, the actress, without any warning, transforms herself into a sage. With a wild look in her eye Tessa exclaims:

*"Some artists never receive recognition in their lives, yet they are always **drawn by their star**. They follow their dream, stay true to their process, even though they have no*

idea where it will lead them. Other artists find a formula and may or may not become rich."

In a nutshell, the actress's spellbinding monologue describes my artist spirit perfectly. *I'm magnetically drawn by a star*, always, everywhere. I feel elated by this explanation of the creative process and—if I can remember it—it will help me to feel OK about myself in the moments when I wonder what I'm doing with my life.

Just as the actress finishes speaking, a tiny bat flies into the kitchen at breakneck speed. It sweeps low and circles many times over our heads. We look up astonished, shielding our eyes, then study each other's expressions. One of us admits quickly to having a bat phobia. My mind works hard to figure out how it's found a way in. Down the chimney I think. The terrified little creature then swoops upstairs into the meditation room which has two doors. It's Dink the plumber who rises to the challenge. When I try to open the window it dive-bombs me. The clown takes over.

"Leave the room," he whispers.

I back out. In the darkness he quietly opens the iron door which leads on to a steep mountain lane. The frightened little messenger swiftly leaves.

In Native American culture the bat heralds a new beginning. This chance encounter with the Irish sage and the clown-turned-plumber leaves me feeling excited and encouraged to tell the stories I found in Patagonia and to write my film. I have my story now and I appreciate that I've always had my guiding star.

That same night, just two days after returning from Chile, an incredible electric storm hits our tiny remote village. Rain lashes, thunder roars, huge hailstones rattle down my unfinished chimney onto the kitchen floor. All the lettuces in the village get pummelled to death.

It's a dramatic beginning to a new chapter in my life and I realise the next day that Patagonia and my film have become a love affair. I'm in this relationship now with all that I have to give. I'm going for gold. And I'll try very hard not to sabotage this dream with doubts, disappointments and the inevitable obstacles that always colour the way. I've found a new life path and I'm ready to write again.

Chapter 1

THE FIRST THING that surprises you when you arrive in Santiago is the number of white faces. Santiago feels European. Germans, Russians and eastern Europeans flocked to Chile before and after the two World Wars. Gutsy pioneers claimed land and built whole villages. Missionaries arrived, Catholicism spread. The indigenous Mapuche and Tehuelches peoples were almost wiped out in the late 19th century by the Spanish, then disease devastated those who were left. The native Tehuelches were big people. It's said that when the Spanish first arrived, they discovered Tehuelche footprints in the sand. "¡Qué patagón!" somebody remarked—"What a large foot!"—and the land became known as Patagonia for ever more.

Before I leave Spain, an astrologer friend cautions me to be extremely careful on the twenty eighth of this month and on day one in Chile, a tarot reader in Santiago warns me that a crisis is coming my way.

I DON'T TRUST THE CHECK-IN GUY at Granada airport when he says my wheelie will go straight through to Santiago, Chile.

"No need to reclaim it in Madrid," he tells me authoritatively.

"But my second flight's with a different airline," I say.

"I'm telling you it's fine," he says impatiently.

How nice to be able to travel with just one small backpack, I think as I then navigate the maze called Madrid Barajas Airport. I wish this was all I needed to bring. So, fourteen hours later in Santiago Airport, I watch the carousel spin the last solitary bag around the slow-moving track, and—surprise, surprise—it's not mine. Hmm, I think. What now?

"Your bag will arrive tomorrow, it will be delivered to your hotel," the friendly LAN Chile employee informs me. Three businessmen are blowing hot and cold beside me having also lost their luggage.

"Are you sure?" I ask.

"Yes, yes," she beams. I ask for a complementary overnight pack, and am given a deluxe blue bag with a razor, shaving cream, deodorant, toothpaste and large white T-shirt. I'm happy to discover I'm not stressed by this little drama.

SANTIAGO HAS BEEN DESCRIBED as the most polluted city in South America. Pollution is the country's biggest environmental problem.

My base, Happy House Hostal[1], is just as I remembered it from my first visit last year. One of the friendly cleaners remembers me. But something's different. What about that deafening constant noise outside? Buses screeching to a halt below every bedroom window till one in the morning, and then starting again at 5.30 a.m.? Where's the noise? Where are all the battered old buses, the fumes, the bustle?

The new, courageous president, single mother of three, Michelle Bachelet, is addressing the problem, but it's not

---

1   Hostal is the spelling used in Spanish, including South American Spanish, so I have retained this throughout the book.

fixed yet. Far from it. With its air trapped in a valley between mountain ranges, Santiago with its five million inhabitants suffers from excessive factory and vehicle emissions, plus dust blown from unpaved roads and eroded hillsides. Over the city hangs a blanket of extremely dangerous smog. One analyst says living in the city is equivalent to smoking 300 cigarettes a day.

Michelle has decided to do something about it. Dusty suburban streets are being vacuumed. Dirt roads paved. The multi-coloured, graffitied old buses have been banned, removed. All of them. There used to be hundreds of private companies running these buses all over the city, filling the air with noise and toxic fumes and life. Without exception, they've been made illegal. Now fleets of brand new vehicles create a new problem. Alarmingly, Santiago finds itself in serious early morning and late afternoon chaos. There are not enough buses to get everybody to work. The underground system is completely overloaded, and people have to queue for hours. A television report shows a tailback of weary commuters about half a mile long waiting to get into the underground. The soundtrack is not a voiceover; there are no words to describe this daily ordeal, just music, which pains my heart as the camera scans the quiet distress of thousands of tired men and women stoically waiting to get home. These people are intimately familiar with the unacceptable.

BY TWO O'CLOCK on day one, before I've seen the TV footage, I find myself in the underground. I've just got off a train. I'm trying to find my way out. There are five exits, and I'm looking for the one leading to the office where I'll buy, I hope, my cheap ticket to Puerto Montt for tomorrow's flight. I'm on a mission. I've yet to meet the tarot reader, so my heart is singing.

Hoards of people are moving in both directions. The old neurosis about having my Visa card stolen makes its annoying little voice heard loudly. The small red embroidered Peruvian money bag which nearly got snatched in the Madrid underground this year dangles snugly underneath my well-travelled orange fleece.

It's summer here but my body still thinks it's in chilly Spain. I'm cold. I clasp my tummy trying not to think *Visa card/thief/big trouble/embassy/hassle/tears/* when I hear a faint angelic voice.

I stop in my tracks and look around. Where's this classical music coming from? A radio? No. Nobody else is stopping. I follow the sound though a long shabby grey tunnel to find a young woman at the foot of the exit stairs, singing her heart out. She's about twenty years old, probably a music student. The acoustics are fantastic. A brown felt hat lies at her feet. She has one of the most beautiful mezzo-soprano voices I've ever heard anywhere. She's a star. The young woman takes no notice of the passers-by, yet she's chosen her spot carefully. Standing a few feet away from her, back to the wall, I close my eyes and drift into her musical world. She's singing '*Ombra mai fu*' the haunting opening love song from Handel's opera Xerxes, popularly known as Handel's Largo, a tale set in Persia in 480BC. After a while, I notice a few young men stopping briefly to listen and look, or maybe to look and listen. The mezzo-soprano is medium height, slim, with short, brown, thick, wavy hair, beautifully plain, undecorated and natural.

The unending crowd moves on and on, up the escalator and out into the summer sunlight, into the busyness of the city. Down here in this concrete sewer-like underworld, music perfumes the air. When the singer stops briefly and I ask her if she knows Rameau's *O Nuit,* the exquisite solo made famous and popular by the film The Chorus.

"No," she says curtly, "I don't."

Swaying gracefully, she disappears once more inside herself, inside her classical music. This time it's Bach. How interesting, hardly anybody is looking at her, yet we all hear her.

I think about all the training and practising she must have done. Is she funding her studies herself? And if she isn't a music student, how has she learnt to sing like this? I visualise her career unfolding. Maybe she's a waitress at night, or a poorly paid singer in a bar? Will she be successful and world famous one day? Or will she be a busker all her life? Or something in-between? What's her story? Is her mother a singer? Is her father an Italian immigrant? A famous baritone? A conductor? A bus driver? Does she have a father? How come she gets such feeling into her music? She's so young to be so heartfelt. Will I make her a character in my film? Then I begin to wonder how much I will give her? She's certainly made my day. If nothing else happens today it's been a magical timeless few moments I'll never forget. How much is that worth? Oh dear, I'm back to this uncomfortable thinking again. I give her a note and immediately wish I'd given her triple.

TEN MINUTES LATER I'm facing an elderly woman in a white, frilly dress meandering slowly down the long, broad, crowded main street. She has a small, black, hairy dog tucked under her arm.

"Excuse me. Do you know where the Sky Airlines office is?" I inquire.

"Yes, round the corner and down to your left."
Wrong.
"Sky Airlines—do you know where the office is please?"
A young man carrying a laptop stops and smiles.
"Yes, straight up and second on the right, first or second on the right."
Wrong.
"Sky Airlines?"
"What?"
"Sky Airlines?"
The next person is a young woman listening to her i-pod. She grins and points behind us. It's here!

The friendly employee commiserates that the website doesn't work overseas; you need a local post code to book a ticket online. She smiles. But yes, a cheap ticket is still available for tomorrow's flight. When would I like to return?

Difficult decision. I feel thrown into conferring with some master plan I am not privy to. I'm here in Chile to find a story. I don't know how long this will take, nor where it will lead me. So I say the fifth of April, the day before Good Friday.

THE SMILING WAITER hands me a plate of salad and chips. I was here at this very same table last year. There's a delicious feeling of familiarity. Within this district of Santiago I know my way around. Two pneumatic drills spring into action just five feet away as I take my first bite of Chilean lettuce. The local clients at this pavement café and the street vendors selling exotic fruits nearby take no notice of the noise and dust. Very soon after I've enjoyed every single mouthful of the luscious chocolate and strawberry dessert, I find myself eyeing the tarot reader. His stall is in the middle of half a dozen others which line one side of the Plaza Brazil.

"Sit down," he says pointing to two old camping stools.

Our knees almost touch. He gives me a pack of well-used cards to shuffle. His eyes are dark brown and intense. Anton's about thirty, serious, thin and interesting. He's also selling esoteric books laid out on a rickety table.

"Ask three questions," he says quietly. Our eyes lock.

A flash of electric sexual energy hits me by surprise. I'm distracted, sidetracked and intrigued. In a split second my imagination has whisked me into Anton's world. I see him living in a dilapidated historic building, a Bohemian ghetto in an unpaved neighbourhood nearby. We've climbed six flights of crumbling staircase to reach his attic hideaway. Now I'm in his studio. It's full of dust covered books and political paintings. It's twilight time. Warm. We're sitting opposite each other on camping stools. There's a little round red table with a bottle of cheap white wine and two empty glasses between us. I notice an open window looking out onto a narrow iron balcony. The sun is a vanishing crimson balloon in a dusky orange sky. I think I can smell jasmine, or is it beer? A church bell chimes. I'm in South America. Our knees touch.

"Your questions?" Anton asks again.

With a blink, my beautiful vision fades as quickly as it arrived. I want to like him but he remains detached, neutral.

He says something about sexuality, expressing it in art; I'm only half listening. What I remember most is the *crisis* he says is coming my way.

"You will learn something very valuable through it," he says.

I try to push for more info but it doesn't come. When, where? And what about finding my story, and writing the film script. Am I going to be successful?

Pause.

Silence.

A seemingly never-ending pause.

"Yes, but it's linked with the crisis, success will come from the story."

Success will come from the story.

We are speaking in Spanish and I wonder what's getting lost in translation. I leave Anton saying I might come back in six weeks, when I've found my story. He smiles, and once again our eyes lock. But five minutes later the whole experience has faded into nothingness, except for the word *crisis*. And sexuality.

Chapter 2

IT'S LATE AFTERNOON now and my head feels itchy. Total luxury is having my hair washed and my head massaged by somebody else. I'll look for a hairdresser. I wander slowly back towards Happy House Hostal reliving the magical and funny moments of the day: the angel in the tunnel, the smiling Sky Airlines assistant with the three wrong sets of directions to find her, the salad covered by cement dust and the tarot reader. I'm thinking it's been a Big Day. But it's far from over yet.

I see red-haired, middle-aged Jeanette though the window of her small salon. It's empty and she's on her mobile.

"How much for a wash and blow dry?" I ask.

"Not much," she says. "Sit down."

I'm thinking *The Story*. I'll start right now, today. I'll ask her how she came to live in Chile. I'm guessing she's an immigrant. I need to start practising asking questions.

Jeanette energetically massages lemon scented shampoo into my scalp. Even though it's more of a pummelling and a thumping, it's bliss. Her hands feel like toy hammers and her crimson nails are a little too long. Everything in the tiny two-sink salon seems to be dull orange or beige. It's so box-like we're practically sitting in the street. We get chatting. Something she says prompts me to tell her I was adopted as a baby. I was born in Ireland I tell her, and was adopted in Scotland in unusual circumstances by unusual people.

"What did your adopted parents do for a living?" she asks thoughtfully, studying me in the mirror.

"They were both doctors."

Jeanette washes off the shampoo with scalding water. Then, vigorously, she rubs a handful of conditioner into my scalp. It smells like disinfectant.

"What kind of doctors? Hospital doctors?"

"One was a hospital doctor the other was a family doctor."

"What ... what ...?"

"What kind of a hospital doctor? Well, since you ask ..."

If I have one skill in life it seems to be the ability to create a safe space for others—men and women—to share easily their deepest concerns, their personal stories and their dreams. I don't know how this is and I don't remember if it was always so. But wherever I find myself in the world, it happens. And sometimes it happens in reverse. Like now. Except that my personal stories are mostly de-fused these days; they don't carry pain. But I'm still shy about discussing the real me. Even with friends I know well, I'd rather hear their tangled tales and hearts' desires than air mine. Maybe this is my greatest personality flaw. I'm secretive, except when travelling

Jeanette rinses off the conditioner with tepid water. She digs her sturdy fingers once more into my skull and pulls hard. My hair squeaks. She picks up an orange towel.

"Entonces—" she says ("So—").

"Entonces," I continue. "My guardians—that's what I called my adoptive parents—were in their forties when they decided to adopt two children. This was in Scotland, in Edinburgh, just after the war. There were many 'war babies' up for adoption and there was no vetting of prospective parents in those days. Single men or single women could adopt as many children as they wanted. Same sex couples could adopt. We knew of a single woman who adopted five orphans. A profession and a house were the only prerequisites as far as I know. So my guardians adopted Andrew first, a baby boy from the island of Skye, whose mother sang in a church choir, then me, half-Jewish Jennifer, from Ireland. They re-named us and gave us the same Scottish surname so that later the world would think, and we would feel, that we were brother and sister. This was a clever idea which back-fired slowly. The reason they didn't give us either of their surnames is a bit too complicated to explain."

"Oh," says Jeanette intrigued. "Why?"

Truth be told, I don't want to share this part of my story with her. I don't want to tell her I was adopted by two women. An old man with very little hair comes into the salon and asks for a haircut.

"Come back in half an hour," Jeanette replies without a smile.

"So," she says, picking up the thread again. "So …?"

"Well, they told me they chose me because I was the skinniest most mal-nourished three month old baby in the orphanage. I also had jaundice which they knew they could cure!"

Later I discovered this was not the whole truth. I was chosen because of my 'back story'. My tiny past. My Jewish history.

The phone rings. Jeanette gets into an animated discussion in French about bingo with her friend Cybelle. I'm glad of this intermission because I've decided to edit my story radically. I want to hear her story. So far all I know about her is that she dies her hair red and that her family came from France.

Five minutes later, still smelling of pine disinfectant with water running down the back of my neck, Jeanette continues her questioning.

"So your mom was a doctor too?"

I pause to let her know I'm going to change the tempo of the story.

"Yes."

Some cold soapy water trickles into my eye.

"What was she like, I mean, was she—?"

"She was an extraordinary woman!"

I used to tell the story that she was the first woman ever to be appointed a consultant at the Edinburgh Royal Infirmary. But she corrected me when she was eighty five. She lived to be ninety four.

"She became the second female consultant for women patients in the pioneering STD department in the Edinburgh Royal Infirmary, that's in Scotland. The first one lasted all of two weeks, she was too domineering. You know what STDs are?"

"No."

We pause while I translate the letters. We're taking in Spanish. My French isn't up to this kind of story telling.

"Madre mia!" she snorts. "Oh yes, I know what you mean."

"So, she became a specialist in sexually transmitted diseases," I continue.

"She worked in a Salvation Army hospital in London during the first world war, delivering babies and caring for the poorest of poor women. She was a surgeon too. I Googled her recently and discovered she had more than twenty letters after her name!"

Jeannette mops some water off my forehead. Our eyes meet in the mirror.

"Another of her passions was illegitimate babies up for adoption. Particularly Jewish babies. All babies from other countries had to be checked for nasty diseases. That's how she met my real mom and heard her story. Her gals— girls—as she called her patients, were mostly brave ladies of the night. My mother wasn't, and she didn't have a nasty disease. Some patients would have been casualties of one night stands, others, unlucky wives of returning soldiers. The worst luck for a baby was being born with your parent's illness."

"What did you call her?" Jeanette seems genuinely curious.

"Well, when I was little I called her mummy, but when I was older I called her Emma. Her initials were MM. She'd always called her beloved partner RMH, so it sort of felt natural. But Emma sounded nicer than MM. More musical. Remember JFK in the sixties?

"Who?"

"J F Kennedy, the American president? Initials have always been popular with certain kinds of people.

"Really?"

Jeanette picks up the hairdryer and the noise now muffles our voices.

"Women doctors had to be very tough and very clever in those days."

I'm almost talking to myself at this point, the noise from the hairdryer gets louder.

"Emma just missed being a suffragette. She qualified as a doctor in 1921. She'd be 107 if she was alive today!"

"Hmmm," sighs Jeanette slowly. I sense she has something to add here but she wants to hear more, so I carry on.

"Well—"

The hairdryer makes too much noise. My voice gets drowned. She seems accustomed to talking over this noise but my voice isn't strong enough, so I pause. We stop the conversation.

Deep in thought, the hairdresser's hands start rummaging roughly through my damp hair, a bit like you might dry a dog's hair after a wet walk in the rain.

Lulled by her silence and the drone of the hairdryer, I slip into a quiet dreamy space for a few moments and remember other bits of information about my adopted mother's interesting life, before I became part of it.

I RECALL THE PHOTO of her aged twenty, playing the cello. Her elegant Victorian mother stands beside her, music in hand, singing. Her older sister grows up to be a talented artist and an acclaimed violinist. There are frequent musical soirées in their household. This is a quintessentially pre-First World War, upper-middle-class English family, complete with high tea in the nursery for the children, strict governesses, i.e. home schooling, servants, groomsmen, gardeners, nannies, cooks, tweenies (maids) and croquet on the lawn. There's also a grass tennis court close to the stables where the doctor's horse and carriage are housed, and there's a boy next door, but he gets killed in the First World War, leaving seventeen year old Emma with just a few sepia photos of himself, and long string of multi-coloured glass beads he bought back from Venice.

JEANETTE STOPS THE HAIRDRYER to hunt for a better one that works without smoking. My mind drifts back to re-examine other images I've saved of Emma's unusual life.

SHE'S CLIMBING THE CULLINS, the mystical, challenging, highest mountains on the island of Skye in Scotland. It's 1930. RMH is with her. They're camping. Camping, climbing and picnicking. Three things they love. They also love babies but aren't able to have any themselves. They've left it too late and anyway, all the nice men got killed in the war they tell me when I ask why they haven't got husbands. They've cycled from Edinburgh. It's quite a few hundred kilometres.

JEANETTE makes noises in the background, still hunting for a hairdryer that doesn't smoke.

MY FAVOURITE PHOTO of Emma is brownish and whitish. 'Summer 1938' is artistically written in black ink on the back. Emma is thirty seven. She's holding a bird, a gannet with a wingspan of two meters; she's just ringed it on the famous Bass Rock. The Bass Rock is a sea bird sanctuary, a tiny island near Edinburgh, said to be one of the wildlife wonders of the world, breeding home to razorbills, puffins, eider ducks and one hundred and fifty thousand gannets. She's smiling a wonderful smile, wearing a longish tweed skirt. She's tall and windswept. Her boobs are large and her blouse is white. Her shoes are study and she's wearing ankle length socks. She is not, of course, yet wearing the gold locket she always wore which had my photo and Andrew's photo in it, because at this stage of things, neither of us exists.

My replacement English mother was an idealist, a cellist, an ace tennis player, a car mechanic, a surgeon, peripatetic prison doctor, mountaineer, lay preacher, medical pioneer, public health campaigner, bird lover, writer of two STD text books, humanitarian and a feminist, though she'd never have called herself a feminist. Emma was splendidly unusual. RMH, her beloved life partner the Scot, the intellectual, the scholar, the angry failed missionary turned atheist, the respected family doctor, was different before I was adopted. Coming from a line of brilliant academics, her harsh, Scottish Calvinistic upbringing and her deeply damaged psyche would not allow her heart to open to an Irish-Dutch-Jewish foundling, and from the start, jealousy insidiously grew into hatred. For RMH—Aram-Aitch, as we pronounced it— little Scottish Andrew was enough. Emma must have loved me much too much. Pre-words, RMH made it crystal clear I was not welcome.

JEANETTE'S MOBILE rings again. Wrong number she mumbles. Now she disappears into the street. The break allows me a final pause for a few more memories to surface before it's her turn to talk.

SUDDENLY, I'VE GOT A WHOLE LITTLE MOVIE playing in my head. I'm walking down the corridor in Emma's STD ward in the Victorian Edinburgh Royal Infirmary. It's 1949. I'm four. I'm sometimes dressed as a miniature nurse. This happens almost every Sunday throughout my childhood. Christmas and Easter included. One Sunday a month we visit the maternity hospital, which is where Emma does her foreign (and Scottish) illegitimate babies with possible nasty diseases clinic. This is where we first met. Sunday morning at the Infirmary is the much revered consultant's 'special' ward round. I'm being taken bed by bed to have my blond curly hair ruffled by Emma's brave 'gals'. She asks each patient how's she's feeling today. I get my cheeks tweaked and sometimes my face caressed. Absolutely no kissing is allowed. Every Sunday my world grows to encompass thirty adoring replacement mothers. I think this ritual is Emma's way of encouraging her ladies to think about getting well and going home. And I think it's my initiation into becoming a doctor, which both Aram-Aitch and Emma have decided I will be. I have different views. I don't even want to be a nurse. Aged four, I decide I want to draw, and explore, for the rest of my life. Nothing more.

Occasionally on Sundays I'm frightened. Some of the ladies are blind. A few are deaf and blind. Some are bandaged. Some have no teeth. Some have rashes. After the ward round, those who can get out of bed sit on chairs in front of the big, black, honky-tonk piano. I'm always looking forward to the juice and biscuits after this bit of the morning, and I love the smell of grown up coffee that fills the corridor. Emma delivers a short religious sermon beside the piano, with a positive and encouraging message, which I discover later she's spent hours writing. A few hymns are sung. Whoever can play four or five chords on the piano gets the job of pianist, usually a nurse, occasionally a patient. Emma has a strong serious leading voice. Not many of the ladies sing. I'm exempt because I can't read till I'm eight. I'm told I'm 'good' because I manage to sit quite still. I adore Emma's junior doctors who work at the hospital for usually just a year, then disappear. These women are always either Indian or Polish/Jewish. I love them because they smell nice and smile a lot. Emma has a tremendous respect for the Jewish people. Even at this tender age she's impressed on my psyche that the Jews are a special race, and that I am extremely fortunate to have had a Jewish father.

Some years later, when I'm no longer sweet but adolescent, moody and sexually curious, I periodically take to exploring the off-limits parts of the ward after the coffee and biscuits. It's Sunday so nobody's around. I love skating, so I skate up the corridors, my school shoes sliding over meters of grey polished floors. I run fingers (which my piano teacher whacks every week) along endless walls of dull, green disinfected tiles. I open cupboards. In the background are hospital noises, telephones ringing, food trolleys arriving, the lift opening and closing. I test the wide swinging entrance doors to the ward, and scrutinise the fleet of vacant wheelchairs. The empty Treatment Room with its metal examination table always covered with a pristine white sheet but no pillow, feels more sinister every time I check it out. Does sex always have to equal disaster? I often peek into the row of dark changing cubicles, not at all like the cubicles at nice friendly swimming pools. These little undressing rooms feel full of ghosts.

I spook myself every time I explore these parts of Emma's life. This drama filled, female-fear filled, end-of-the-line place where my courageous replacement mother works tirelessly and with such compassion. Emma still expects me to become a doctor. I know this will never happen. Aged fifteen, I'm on the brink of deciding to become a successful writer. Or maybe a poet. Or possibly an actress! Aram-Aitch thinks I'm the most ignorant Irish-Jewish idiot/disaster on the planet.

The STD ward becomes ingrained in my teenage mind as a fate worse than death. In the 1980s, between marriages, when I turn up as I patient for a check up in another STD clinic, I discover it's a friendly place with super-sensitive nurses and sexy doctors wearing fishnet stockings. They've all studied Emma's text books.

"DID YOU EVER FIND your real, Irish mum?" Jeanette asks as she restarts to blow-dry my hair with another antique hair dryer. She stares at me in the mirror again, scrunching my hair and roasting the back of my neck with too much heat.

"Yes," I tell her, wriggling to escape having my ears singed. I give her a postage stamp sized version of my story. She remains quiet for a while.

"We have a secret in our family too," she says.

Then she tells me her story.

JEANETTE'S FAMILY emigrated from France three generations ago. She is proud to be French and visits France once a year. Around the time the Eiffel Tower was being built her great-grandmother, a ravishing beauty, sailed from France and arrived in Chile with her young engineer-architect husband. But she hated Santiago and quickly grew to hate her husband too. Around the year the Eiffel Tower was opened (1889) she sailed back to France alone. On the boat she met another engineer, a distant relation of Gustave Eiffel, the designer of the Eiffel Tower. They fell in love. The Eiffel family were extraordinary people of Russian-German origin. Gustave designed not only the Eiffel Tower, the Statue of Liberty, the main train station in Santiago and countless bridges and civic buildings worldwide; he also invented the suspender belt! Engineers were changing the world. The young couple were wealthy.

After a short sojourn in Paris, Jeanette's great-grandmother and her lover returned to Santiago where she gave birth to a son. Nobody knows who the father of the child is: the husband or the lover. That child, Jeanette's great uncle, died many years ago but the family now wants an answer. So at this very moment in time, relations are scouring the records in Paris for his birth certificate, which nobody has ever seen.

MY HAIR IS NOW DRY and Jeanette's husband arrives. Everything changes. To my surprise she switches off the connection we've just made, and becomes a stranger.

"Four hundred pesos," she says briskly. Four euros. No goodbye.

I buy some fresh vegetables for supper from the busy supermarket across the road, and return to Happy House Hostal with a vivid picture of a period costume movie running through my head, and some strong stirred up memories which may be useful for themes for my screen play.

Although it's only day one, I've already collected a few interesting characters for my story. I've got an angel in a dingy tunnel with a small amount of money in brown felt hat. A mysterious tarot reader who warns of a crisis. A hairdresser in a tiny orange salon with a fascinating family story. And I have a theme of not being welcome in the world and a personality flaw of being too secretive.

Is my film in here somewhere? Can I connect these people to tell a new story with a topical theme that will touch hearts, make people smile, and above all, tell a story of real compassion?

Chapter 3

I'VE HEARD THAT Patagonia has cool summers and mild winters. In the south there is no real summer and winters are rarely severe. But there are frequent storms, and sea travel can be extremely treacherous, all year round.

EARLY THE FOLLOWING MORNING, our plane lands at Puerto Montt Airport with a series of bumps and thuds. People clap! It's raining. Actually, it's pouring.

I ring my carefully chosen hostal in scenic, nearby Puerto Versa. It's run by a Scandinavian couple who offer free airport pick-up. I'm anticipating a painted, wooden house full of tasteful Swedish folk art and nice baking smells. They describe their hostal as a mixture of Chilean and Scandinavian flair, *located in a charming street right alongside the city park.* A healthy breakfast of muesli, fruit and freshly brewed coffee is offered. I call the number.

"No pick-up," says an unfriendly female voice.

"But it says free pick-up in the guidebook," I say.

"Yes—but not today."

"How do I get to you then?"

"Taxi!"

The greedy taxi meter rockets as we tear though flat, grey countryside. The rain lashes. I'm cold, hungry and tired. Puerto Veras, close to Puerto Montt, is said to be a lovely place to stop a night or two. Suddenly, travelling shows its unpleasant face. It's not all scenic views and interesting people. This is like Scottish weather at its worst. I'm disorientated and slightly jet-lagged.

When the taxi arrives at Hostal Malmö at about nine o'clock (rather early, I know), I meet Hilda, one of the two young German girls who are running the guest house in the absence of its owners. She's also tired.

"You got the taxi OK?" she asks.

"Of course," I say. "Not a problem," though a bit of an expensive disappointment, I'm thinking.

The wooden house is three storied, dingy yellow outside, slightly drab inside. No folk art. No nice freshly brewed coffee smells as promised. Hilda plods up two flights of narrow wooden stairs and shows me to my tiny room which is under the eaves. The used sheets are whipped off the bed in two seconds and new ones replaced.

"Here you are," she says handing me a large key for the padlock on the door. The skylight is miniature and open, and through it I see a grey, soaking sky and part of a beautiful old pine tree. Not quite the description I had from the guidebook: *"Three snow-capped volcanoes can be seen across the vast expanse of water; on a cloudless night with a full moon, the snows reflect eerily in the lake and the peace and stillness are hard to match".*

I flop onto my new bed and study the peeling paint on the wooden walls. This is a shoebox-sized room. The price is crazy for what it is. Somehow I feel intimidated by the grumpiness of this young woman, so I'm not going to argue about the deal. It's not one of my life skills anyway. OK, I think, just one night here, not two.

AN UNFORGETTABLE SMILE greets me as I explore the downstairs of the hostal. The smile belongs to Jason, who introduces himself as an American wilderness and fishing guide. He spends his summers in Alaska. Now he's looking for somewhere warm to winter. He's searched Chile and southern Argentina up and down for the perfect place, but hasn't found it yet. Jason's about twenty six, medium height, tanned, has a completely shaved head; a tiny trendy beard under a thin bottom lip.

"Where are you heading?" he asks after some preliminary chatting, his eyes shining, unblinking.

"Tortel," I say.

"How are you gettin' there?" He seems genuinely interested.

"I'm hoping to get the ferry from Puerto Montt down to Chacabuco. It's about a three-day sail. Then it'll be local minibuses inland," I explain carefully.

He's still interested.

"I've read the ferry journey is amazing," I tell him. I'm not used to giving detailed plans to anybody but he quizzes me more, so I continue.

"The boat sails slowly in between thousands of little islands, it's a cargo boat, and it's usually full of mooing cattle."

Jason laughs, his smile slowly fades.

"You sure there's a ferry?"

"Well yes—no!" I'm not sure at all.

"If the ferry runs, it'll take about a week to get to Tortel," I tell him. "If it isn't running or is full, which sounds possible, I'll have to get various buses down through Argentina, then zigzag south. That'll take much longer. It's very hard to get information about this ferry!"

"I know," says Jason. "It's hard to get info about any form of transport in this country. Tomorrow, I'm splashing out and taking a small plane to Chaiten, it's not that expensive and it's so much quicker. Distances are vast here." He's still smiling. He's not short of cash.

"This your first visit to Chile?" he asks.

"No, it's my second."

Chaiten could be on my way to Tortel. It's just one of the many possible ways to get there. I could go that way too, tomorrow. But I prefer to arrive slowly. It's not the money that's stopping me catching a plane. I'm financing this trip with my small pension, plus the sale of a painting, plus the money I've earned from my last paying guests.

Jason then paints a graphic picture of his next adventure, starting with the forty minute flight in an eight-seater plane. He'll then catch a small minibus to a magical place called Futaleufú. He's also a kayak and rafting instructor. *Futa* is one of the world's top three white water rafting centres, he informs me.

"The other two are in Spain and Africa."

"I know," I say.

I tell him I've spent two summers painting near the Spanish one. It's in the Pyrenees. Jason tells me he's planning to go to Africa soon. He's heard the fishing's great in this unpronounceable place called Futaleufú and he's hoping maybe this could be his winter home.

Both of the Amazonian German girls who are looking after the hostal are madly—madly being the word—in love with a small Argentinean who wears a white ski cap with a red bobble. That's why they're both angry. This is Jason's next story. The Argentinean lives in the loft, smokes a lot of dope and plays his guitar all day.

"He's playing one against the other." Jason laughs loudly.

All three are living in the attic above the eaves.

"Have you been to Tortel?" I ask him as he relinquishes the seat in front of the computer to me.

"No," he says, "I haven't. But I've heard about it."

INDEPENDENT TRAVEL in South America takes a lot of planning and considerable mental energy. There are always so many possibilities. Patience and flexibility are essential. Impatience and fixed ideas lead to various states of acute anxiety or real lingering disappointment and huff.

So, when later in the morning a young man arrives to work in the hostal office, I ask his help in booking my ferry passage. Both German the girls have disappeared. The loft is quiet.

Antonio is about twenty three, slim, kind-faced and slightly shy. He's from Puerto Veras but, strangely, he knows next to nothing about the maritime system in his country. He does his best to find out about the ferry situation. After a few hours we come up against the same obstacle I discovered in Santiago. There is a ferry, two actually, but one sank recently. Well almost sank. It's being repaired. Now all the bookings are being jumbled up. They're trying to fit two lots of bookings into one ferry.

"The only way you might get a ticket," Antonio informs me seriously, "is to turn up at midnight at the dock tomorrow. If somebody doesn't turn up, you can buy their ticket."

This is the official advice. Too bad if it's the most expensive ticket. The ferry runs once every ten days.

"What if I get buses down to Tortel and then catch the ferry back to Puerto Montt? Can I book that?" I ask Antonio.

No. It doesn't look like it.

"Why?"

"Because the other ferry, the one that's being repaired, may not be ready by then."

"But what about the one that is working?"

"No."

Umm. "Why not?" I lose the thread then. I'm fixated on the idea of travelling long distances by boat. I seem to be determined to get this ferry one way or the other. Perseverance and more information will surely win the day?

"Have you been to Tortel?" I ask this serious young man.

My quiet new friend shakes his head and looks apologetic.

"No, never. Never heard of it. You sure it's in Chile?"

A friendly smile concludes our two hour relationship of frustrating phone calls. I retreat to the kitchen to see Jason smoking on the deck outside with one of the German girls. Hilda's slurping a tall glass of steaming hot chocolate, and smoking a tad frantically. She gives me a black, back-off look and Jason grins. It's a bit of a pantomime, this love triangle. Is Jason now part of it I wonder? Doesn't look like it. I remind myself with a little smile that I know something about her she doesn't know I know! She scowls at me. I feel ridiculously wounded. I leave them watching the colourless drizzle cover the newly-cropped lawn.

STUDYING THE MAP I see the overland route to Tortel will take me through Bariloche in Argentina. So, I need to check the bus times. Puerto Veras is supposed to be a delightful spot but today it's not. It's cloaked in this dense, grey Scottish drizzle, and the German love drama is disturbing me way too much. I don't feel welcome here. The house is full of bad energy according to Jason, but strangely it doesn't seem to be affecting him. I'm glad to go out for a walk.

At the bus depot I'm told there's one ticket left for tomorrow's departure. I sign the papers, give my passport number and am told to be at the bus station at 6.15 a.m. It will be a nine hour journey.

BACK IN MY GARRET BEDROOM I begin to revise my plan. No ferry, so bus to Bariloche, through Argentina, stay overnight in Bariloche. Next day, El Bolsón, a beautiful village in a valley surrounded by mountains. Hippies from Buenos Aires settled there in the 1970s. They formed a kind of utopian community and many artists, writers and healers live there still. It sounds interesting.

Suddenly I'm almost jolted off my bed by a tremendous crash on the landing outside my room. I fling the door open and find Hilda heaped like a discarded glove puppet at the bottom of the stepladder which leads to the upper loft, the love nest! She's fallen down (slipped or pushed?) but insists she's absolutely fine. Guitar music continues to play from above. She then locks herself in the only bathroom for the next forty five minutes.

Jason tells me more about Futaleufú and its turquoise river. I look it up on the internet. Two rivers meet here, the Futa and the Azul. From the satellite map I see alluring Prussian-blue lakes punctuating forest-clad, snow-dusted mountain ranges. It's a vast chunk of wilderness, impossible to tame, no mobile phone masts here. No telegraph poles. No supermarkets, no gas station, no quad bike tours. There's only one road in and out of the village.

Later that night Jason hugs me goodbye. I'm sorry to say adios to this ray of sunshine in damp and grey Puerto Veras.

Chapter 4

IN CHILE, the monkey puzzle tree is known as the umbrella or parasol tree. The species has flourished here for two hundred million years. This extraordinary tree grows slowly and can live for twelve hundred years. I can't begin to understand how experts can fathom this out, but this is what I've read. The umbrella tree has always been revered by the native Mapuche people, who still leave offerings to the tree's spirit at certain times of the year.

LONG DISTANCE JOURNEYS BY BUS in Chile usually start early in the morning or late at night. Our bus sets off at 6.30 a.m., almost full. I'm hoping we're going to see lots of parasol trees. We pick up a few passengers en route. Quite soon we reach the Chilean border and the customs ritual begins. I'm used to this procedure now, but this time it's different. Our driver wants us lined up in alphabetical order outside the customs building. He has all our passports and papers, but he can't find my name on his list.

I'm not on the list. He becomes nervous, even though I have all the papers he needs.

"Stand at the end of the line," he tells me.

A long chat takes place between him and the army personnel when it comes to my turn to be exited from Chile. They keep looking at me. Everybody else is back in the bus.

Finally I'm stamped and cleared and off we drive through no-man's-land till we reach the Argentine border.

The same thing happens again as we queue to enter Argentina. Our anxious middle-aged driver parks the bus, tells us to get out and line up alphabetically.

"Stand at the end," I'm told again.

This time our bus is searched by dogs. They sniff my wheelie and I'm told to take it out of the hold and open it by the roadside.

I start to feel a little panicky because I didn't declare the nuts, seeds, dried fruits and sparklers I brought into the country because I didn't actually reclaim my bag at the airport. How am I going to explain that in Spanish? I could have brought anything into Chile, the way my bag arrived.

The top pocket of my wheelie doesn't lock. Could somebody have slipped something into it at the bus station? Am I going to get taken away and interrogated? Fined? Deported? Is this the crisis the tarot reader predicted? I'm feeling decidedly nervous rehearsing various speeches. The dogs sniff wildly though my clean clothes. Somebody else is asked to open their bag beside mine.

"Take this out," a voice tells me. I remove a few layers and the dogs lose interest.

We pile back into our bus and continue the journey. Now we're travelling through a vast, beautiful region known as the Argentine Lake District. Forested mountains rise up from deep indigo lakes. Bariloche, where the journey ends, is reputed to be an extremely popular tourist centre for trekking and sailing.

We pass pretty holiday chalets, Swiss style, dotted infrequently across the lush green countryside. Sprawling, flower-filled villages appear intermittently. This is the land of the ancient monkey puzzle tree where you can walk in the perfectly preserved footprints of dinosaurs, so my *Footprints* guidebook tells me. I think I'll have to come back because there are no umbrella trees or footprints to be seen from the bus.

As we approach Bariloche, we look down on a mass of neat, wooden houses wedged around the curve of a grey lake. It's still raining. I feel a huge NO filling my chest. NO. I don't want to stay here. How can this possibly be? This 'No' voice is serious. I think it's what the Quakers call the 'still small voice inside us'. It's our intuition.

We arrive at about four in the afternoon. It's been a long drive. I leave the bus with the NO getting stronger. No, I don't want to stay the night in a tourist chalet hotel. But why not? Just one night?

As usual a trip to the ladies' toilet gives the Universe time to slip Plan B into place, and on the way out, I see a ticket booth selling tickets to El Bolsón, my destination for tomorrow.

"When's the next bus leaving?" I ask curiously.

"In twenty minutes," I'm told.

"And how long will it take?"

"A few hours."

Smiling, I buy my ticket and feel elated.

THE NEXT FOUR HOURS are pure heaven. The landscape becomes wilderness, no interference of any sort by humans. We are driving right alongside the Andes. Quickly, I find myself in a state of pure awe. It's like seeing the northern lights for the first time, the beauty is almost overwhelming.

For the last year, El Bolsón has been luring me like Tortel, but in a less extreme way. There's some interesting art being made here. I've read it's a magical place surrounded by mountains dominated by one massive peak, with a river running through the valley and a warm, sunny microclimate.

As we approach the village, I am dismayed to feel that familiar NO rearing its little head again. El Bolsón is a sprawling rural community. It spreads out over miles and miles. You need a car to live here. By now I'm exhausted and a bit stumped. Our twelve-seater bus stops by the busy post office. I get out and begin to study the guidebook for a bed for the night.

"La Casa de Babette: charming wooden cabins beside a stream surrounded by an idyllic lavender farm. Delicious home cooking by the charismatic Babette. Reserve ahead," it warns. *"Recommended."*

With the help of a beautiful young man with a long, brown ponytail I phone the number. A neutral male voice answers. "Yes, we have a cabin free for tonight. Take a taxi."

It's not going to be a cheap night. The room is expensive and the taxi driver tells me it's a long way from the village. I'm wondering how I'm going to manage for six weeks if my budget gets stretched too often.

The bruised and dented old taxi swerves off the main road and bangs and wallops down a rutted dirt track. We bounce up and down on our seats. If I wasn't so tired I'd be giggling. The driver is friendly and talks non-stop about El Bolsón and what I should see here.

The landscape is a little like a Wild West film set, but maybe I've been reading too much about Butch Cassidy and the Sundance Kid. They went into hiding just seventy kilometres south of El Bolsón. In the 1969 movie Butch and Sundance get gunned down by the Bolivian army, but rumours have persisted that having faked their deaths, they returned to the USA. Butch was said to have become a businessman, a rancher, a trapper and a Hollywood movie extra, while Sundance had run guns in Mexico, migrated to Europe, fought for the Arabs against the Turks in the First World War, sold mineral water, founded a religious cult, and still found time to marry Etta. This was all around 1901.

Through the taxi window the landscape looks sepia-coloured; everything's fading slowly into evening light. Tumbledown weathered shacks, a dry riverbed with enormous boulders, horses grazing untethered, ragged dirty children playing in the distance. Then suddenly we come to an arty, hand-painted sign by a clump of eucalyptus trees. In unmistakable French script it reads 'Casa Babette'. We have arrived at the lavender farm, and we are exactly fifteen minutes by taxi from the village.

MY FIRST IMPRESSION of Babette is that she is a little more suspicious than charismatic, but soon I'm charmed. My rustic cabin is an enchanting little two-storied house over-looking a stream with lavender all around. Babette is a multi-talented artist. She oozes creativity. Petite, stylishly dressed, long blond hair wrapped up in an exotic headscarf, lots of makeup. She's turned into an interior designer these days it seems, and an acclaimed cook.

"No, the guy who answered the phone is just a good friend," she says. "Not my husband. No husband, but I have many good friends." Smiling, she raises her pencilled eyebrows and the corners of her pretty, crimson mouth. She looks like a woman Toulouse Lautrec would have loved to draw.

The main house where meals are served is chic and obviously the house of a creative person. Babette's paintings and life drawings line every wall. Dried herbs hang from the kitchen ceiling. Baskets of fruit and nuts sit on interesting bits on kitchen furniture. Having many food allergies, I regretfully decline Babette's invitation to supper. I've brought my own healthy food supplies.

THE NEXT MORNING, exploring the land around the house, I find it's pretty much fenced in. Fenced in Patagonia? Beside the stream, a small scruffy dog befriends me. We walk together. I smell the lavender, he smells everything else.

A walk into town takes a good hour, and then a bus to the local National Park takes me to a lake and a little drama with some local customs officials. This National Park is centred round a turquoise lake, Largo Puelo, right on the border with Chile. It's surrounded by evergreen beech forests and acres of cypresses. To reach the park the bus travels past small farms growing walnuts, hops and fruit. Just inside the park there's the entrance to the Forest of Shadows, a wonderfully overgrown copse through which wooden walkways lead to a silvery shingle beach.

The lake is a playground for rich fishermen. For a price, local entrepreneurs whisk their clients out in an assortment of boats, some old, some new. They fish round the corner of the lake, which is in Chile. You need a passport to go fishing here because there's a good chance you'll get blown ashore on the wrong side of the lake.

I watch as a boatload of tourist fishermen get stranded on a sand bank. Their boat starts to keel over. The two customs officials and the local skipper of a pleasure boat rush to the rescue. They untie a rubber government dingy and try to start the engine. No luck. The fishermen are about to hit the water. The resourceful pleasure-boat captain, bare-footed, jumps into another little craft, whisks the engine into life and, joined by a teenager hauling a long rope, speeds to the rescue. They throw the line to the agitated fishermen. It doesn't look like it's going to be possible to right the boat, but when it finally edges free, I'm the one on the jetty clapping! Back on shore the captain winks at me for the third time and tries to persuade me again to take the next excursion with him. He sips his *mate* (a local drink), smiles and disappears out of my life.

At the lavender farm a few hours later, sixty year old Babette tells me she's just had a back operation, the same one I had many years ago. She leans forward and whispers this information. She whispers a lot.

"Was yours a success?" she asks.

"Yes," I tell her, "but I couldn't walk for almost a year!"

"Oh, mon Dieu!" she exclaims. "How terrible! How old were you then?"

"I was nearly thirty. I'd divorced my first husband two years before. It was my worst nightmare to be seriously ill. I had two young children to look after, a full time job and no family to help. It was amazing how many wonderful friends I discovered I had."

"Why you not have a family?" She whispers in broken English. We're sitting in the garden surrounded by lavender. Babette offers me a glass of wine and waits for my answer.

"Well, it's a long story." I try to avoid the question.

"J'adore les histoires," she purrs. And I begin to think she may have a secret past too, but I'm not feeling inclined to share mine, so I don't tell her how I lost my 'parents' by clashing with my guardian Emma just before my eighteenth birthday.

"My parents were too old to help me," I tell her. And this was true.

"Et tu ex? 'Ee was not, how ewe say, kind, 'elp-fool?"

"No," I say, "he was not. Au contraire!"

Prompted by Babette's innocent question, my mind pulls me back into the archives of my life, when Emma and I lost faith in each other, before the back operation. It's all tied up with a love affair. If I share it with Babette, will it open her Pandora's Box? I'm not sure.

"So?" she prompts.

My heart is telling me to guard these delicate memories carefully. So I say I'll be back in a minute and disappear. Walking back to my enchanted cabin through waist high lavender, memories begin to swarm.

IT'S 1963. I'M EIGHTEEN. I've fallen so deeply in love with a penniless, divorced poet, twice my age, that I give up my art college studies in London to live with him in Edinburgh.

The relationship fires the writer in me. I have many poems published at this time. I believe I've found my life's partner, my soul mate, my mentor. This is a horrible, unwise liaison, Emma informs me. You are much too young and he is much too old. If you don't leave him immediately I'll disinherit you. I'm disinherited. Three weeks after moving in with the poet, he falls in love with somebody else, and asks me to leave. I never tell my guardian I've been dumped. Emma leaves my life for the next few years. A psychiatric hospital becomes my new home for the following three months. It has bars on the windows. This is where I first learn to laugh. This is where I find a temporary family. This is where I make a special new friend. Ian is a loveable, charming alcoholic, a fisherman from the island of Skye.

We kiss beside the rhododendron bushes in the beautiful landscaped hospital ground, and every day, no matter what time we arrange to meet, we're interrupted by the bearded old man who wants to know where the post box is. He tells us he's a KGB agent on a mission; that he has an urgent letter which must be posted to President Khrushchev immediately. This catapults us into hysterical laughter. At night, befriended by Ian's group of alcoholic patients, I jump the hospital wall with them and visit seedy bars in Fife, until one night, one of us dies in car crash. After this, Ian goes downhill, and we all stop sneaking out anywhere. Around this time my poetry attracts the attention of a celebrated English poet who is also an elderly Dominican monk. He travels a long distance to visit me in the hospital, and tells me my poet lover has married. He encourages me warmly to keep on writing. I have a special gift, he says.

Three months later I leave the hospital to resume my painting studies, this time at Edinburgh Art College. I find myself vulnerable, voiceless and heartbroken. The painting magic doesn't work for me here. The teaching is too traditional, too conservative after the excitement of London. But my youthful energy and passion to enter the art world gives me a reason to keep on exploring, keep on drawing, keep on writing, and keep on believing in the creative process as the only real life path for myself.

Not long after I restart my studies, I hear Ian has drowned at sea. A belief that love equals tragedy takes root in my heart, and gets played out for the next thirty two years.

One Sunday, the warden at the art college hostel which is now my home, takes me to Roslin Chapel near Edinburgh, where legend says the Holy Grail lies buried in the Apprentice's pillar, a stone column carved by young hands hundreds of years ago.

Father Roland, the priest, lives in a shack of a dwelling near the chapel which he shares with a group of recovering alcoholic men. Father Roland interests me in God.

I RETURN TO BABETTE in her well-kept, flower-filled garden and she refills her glass. A car horn sounds. Somebody's arrived.

"I'll be right back," she whispers. "Don't go away again."

The gay couple from Buenos Aires who have just arrived for two nights seem unfriendly, but Babette works her magic on them. She pours them large glasses of good red wine. Our previous conversation is forgotten. Soon the young men are strutting around the lavender bushes laughing, admiring the large, orange fish in the small, brown pond, smelling the white roses, while creative Babette is busy in the kitchen, preparing a delicious dinner, just for them.

Something's not right for me here at the lavender farm. I feel fenced in. Tortel swims vividly into my awareness. Wild. Cut off from the rest of the world until three years ago. Only accessible by boat down a turquoise river; a five hour, dramatic journey. Boardwalks. Pioneer, self-sufficient people. Far south. Extreme. Attractive to *real* explorers. Hmm. I'm zapped by this place, so tomorrow morning I'll catch the bus to Esquel. What is it about wilderness and wild life and mountains that ignites this passion and lures me to these far flung places without the slightest reservation? It's a question I don't seem to need to answer at the moment. It just is so. It must be in my blood—or is it my Karma? Maybe one day I'll be able to say, it's simply this, or it's simply that.

Later, when we meet again, Babette tells me in her delicious French accent,

"Esquel ees not ewer kind of place Margarita. Bettair ewe stop at Trevelyn. Ewe get eento ze National Park zaire. 'Eets a verraih nice place. I 'ave lots of arteest friends 'eere. Why ewe not stay a leeddle beet longair?"

"No, thank you," I reply. "I don't think so. I have to get to Tortel."

It's difficult to explain why I have to leave. There may well be a fascinating story here to discover. But it's the voice again. And that star. I'm being drawn by my star. We are two different kinds of artists. I think she's tame where I'm wild, and vice versa. I don't sense I'm going to get *the* story out of Babette. She's too interested in domestic things now, cooking, nursing her back. I'm looking for, but not that consciously, a fascinating character with a life challenge and a serious personality flaw that will have to be overcome in order to resolve a topical plot. The only flaw I can see in Babette is that she whispers. She seems to have lost her voice. Why? I'm not taking many notes at this stage of the journey. And I've forgotten to bring the index cards that all the good writing books tell wannabe writers to carry. I'm doing it my way. I'm an artist first and a writer second, so I gather my stories visually, just as I gather my painting images. I follow my intuition. Soak in impressions.

THE EVENING MEAL IS OVER. The couple from Buenos Aires have gone to bed. From my cabin window I watch Babette hobble across the lawn to her separate house, slightly bent, rubbing her back. The scent of the lavender and jasmine is intoxicating. Watching her, I remember my own convalescence. It's when I write my first TV play. It turns out to be a satirical hospital drama, a black comedy, based on my experiences of acute loneliness and a sense of losing my identity in hospital.

Writing this movie is going to be a different process.

So far in my story gathering I've found a gifted, twenty year old mezzo-soprano busker in a dingy tunnel, a bohemian thirty year old tarot reader who warns of a crisis, a fifty year old red-haired hairdresser with a secret in a poky orange salon, a charming young wilderness guide searching for a winter home amongst people. And I've netted a handsome, middle aged, winking pleasure-boat captain and sexy, sixty year old Babette, who can only whisper. I've unearthed a theme of not being welcome in the world and a personality flaw of being too secretive. I need an obstacle, a mentor and a few allies. Could I hook up Babette with the winking pleasure-boat captain? Or Babette with the tarot reader? Possible. Could Jeanette the hairdresser be the long-lost mother of the singer in the tunnel?

NEXT MORNING the half-full bus leaves early for Esquel. On arriving, the NO voice immediately makes itself felt again. In the bus depot I get to the tourist desk just in time to find out there's a bus leaving for Futaleufú at four o'clock. The next bus will leave in three days. Futaleufú is a white water rafting centre in Chile. It's en route for Chaiten, the ferry port, my gateway to the south. Esquel is in Argentina.

Chapter 5

ARGENTINA has a long tragic past. In January 2002 Eduardo Duhalde became the country's fifth president in two weeks. The country faced bankruptcy, the middle class was devastated. Many lost their life savings. There was widespread poverty and terrible child malnutrition. Sobering to think this was just a few years ago.

I BUY MY TICKET TO FUTALEUFÚ and am told we will arrive at seven in the evening. I find this name impossible to pronounce or remember—it's something like Fout-ta-leyo-foo. A quick look through the guidebook, a phone call to Hospedaje Alfonso and I have a bed booked for the night. Hospedaje means simple accommodation in somebody's home.

"How will I find you?" I ask a young voice.

"Oh, the bus will drop you at the door," I'm told.

"Really?" I ask. "Are you sure?"

Hospedaje Alfonso is described as "*nice and friendly but basic*".

THE JOURNEY FROM ESQUEL to the Chilean border is exhilarating. Babette was right, the National Park is amazing. Our rutted road winds through virgin forests alongside raging, opal-coloured rivers and passes emerald lakes with the snow-capped Andes almost always in full view. We are skirting one of the most magnificent and untouched national parks in Chile. The park was established to protect the tall and stately alerce trees that grow deep in the rainforest.

The bus is a twenty-seater oldie. We drop local people off along the way. A young Israeli couple and I are the only foreigners. By the time we get to the Argentinean border there are just four of us left, including the driver.

We're leaving Argentina now, so nobody's very interested in us it seems. Suddenly it transpires that there is some major misunderstanding, as our bus driver waves goodbye and heads off back to Esquel. What now? We're stranded. Abandoned. It's getting dark. We're left confused at the roadside beside a solitary white mini van. We behave like three sheep who've just realised they've lost the flock. The customs office on the hill looks like an ancient stone cow shed, which it probably was once upon a time. A middle-aged man wearing jeans, a warm grey jersey and the faintest of smiles appears and tells us to get our passports checked.

"Then throw your bags into the van." He disappears.

'We' now consist of a nervous, middle-aged Argentinean woman who seems to have appeared out of thin air, the Israeli couple and me. Twenty minutes later we arrive in the white van at the Chilean customs. It's practically dark now. Our serious driver with the faint smile is extremely shy. The Argentinean woman is a nervous wreck. I'm wondering what's going on. It's completely dark now. A moonless night, to boot.

A portly policeman studies my Irish passport slowly.

"Who is the Irish president right now?" he asks me. I go weak at the knees because I haven't a clue. He watches my face.

"When did the troubles begin in Ireland?"

Our driver looks at me. I remain silent. In the five years since I claimed my Irish citizenship, this is the first time I've felt uncomfortable having an Irish passport. I'm ignorant of almost everything to do with Ireland (having been adopted and grown up in Scotland). I'm not sure whether the customs official, this arrogant soldier, is flirting or playing a game with me, or suspicious that I have a false passport. The Argentine woman is behaving as if she has a false passport. I then notice she hands over a scrap of paper. No passport at all. An expensive jeeps pulls up and a family of well-heeled Americans joins our queue. The father and grandfather look like seasoned fishermen. They've lost their car rental papers so they may not be allowed entry.

As we leave the customs post, followed by the Americans, our Argentinean woman becomes even more edgy. We cross a bridge ten minutes later and arrive in the unpronounceable Futaleufú.

It's inky dark now but the sky is full of sparkling stars. Our driver stops at the brightly-lit bus depot, another wooden shack, and helps our distressed lady with her bag. The bus feels different without her anguish. When he returns I ask if Hospedaje Alfonso is nearby. Yes, he says, I'll take you there now. The exhausted Israeli couple have decided to tag along with me. It feels like I've found two motherless five year olds.

A few minutes later, the door to Hospedaje Alfonso opens and I am overjoyed to see Jason sitting in front of a computer beside a huge wood burning stove. He jumps up and envelops me in a wonderful hug. I had completely forgotten he was coming to Futaleufú. He beams at me once again.

"What a lovely surprise," he says. "What a coincidence. Of all the hostals in the village, and there are many, we have chosen the same one."

The owner's son shows us our rooms. The house is like all the others in the village, made of wood, about fifty years old with chickens running around outside, and apple and pear trees everywhere. No fences here. The wooden floors creak, the beds are narrow, the hot water manages at best to get tepid, but it's wonderfully friendly and welcoming.

MARTA IS THE OWNER of Hospedaje Alfonso. She's a school teacher. Aged about forty five, medium height with short, grey hair and a serious expression, she's the deputy head of the local primary school. I soon discover she's a widow with four grown-up children. A photo of her pilot husband (Alfonso) perches on the kitchen cabinet. He died over twenty years ago. She doesn't elaborate.

The following day Marta's house ebbs and flows with tides of local adults and children. All her visitors are greeted like loved family members. Her serious expression quickly melts. There's no fuss, no great noise. People stream in and out like interesting flotsam and jetsam. She cuddles the children and they squeak in Spanish. Tea is made. Biscuits are shared. Phone calls are made. Letters are read out. The house is alive with village life. I notice they all arrive with quiet expressions, but leave chattering and laughing.

During a lull in visitors, we chat about the things we have in common, grown-up kids, teaching, having been a single parent. Marta tells me a heart-warming story about her daughter who survived all medical odds to recover from a rare blood disease and marry. I tell her about my boys— the multi-talented, younger son who loves to travel and climb mountains, who has become a wonderful father; the older, who is extremely clever and capable of great kindness. And

I tell her proudly I'm learning to be a grandmother to three little beings.

Jason's mood has changed. He hasn't caught a single fish in the three days he's been here. He's dejected and depressed.

"Not a single thing," he protests. "These rivers are fished out," he complains, and he's had a bad reception from the local (American) rafting company.

"They refused to rent *me* a kayak!! 'You gotta go with a tour,' they told me. 'I wanna go alone,' I said. 'Well, at least let me buy a kayak and sell it back to you?' 'Not possible, man,' they said."

The white-water guides are tired after a busy season and worried about insurance. Marta overhears part of the conversation and says the husband of her colleague at school is a fisherman and he'll take Jason to a river where only local people fish. They could go tomorrow afternoon. Jason looks sceptical but agrees politely. That's when Alyssa arrives.

Once more the front door opens to greet yet another world traveller and our little, newly-found family grows. Thirty five year old, blond, smiling, athletic, Australian Alyssa has arrived from Chaiten and, like some messenger in days gone by, she gives us reports of the ferries and information about the Round House at Chaiten, where she's come from today.

IT'S TWO THIRTY and I'm making tea in the kitchen when Marta comes back from school.

"Try mine," she says. "Or better still, try a glass of our local red wine."

She shows me the label and assures me it's terrific. We sit on wobbly wooden chairs with the kitchen door open.

I notice the apple and pear trees in her garden. I see her son's empty, white house-paint pots. I admire the well stacked wood pile. Winter is slowly edging closer here. We sit in silence for a while. My eye keeps getting drawn to the photo of her husband on the dresser. I'd love to know more about him and their life together. She seems to have the same idea.

"Was your first husband an artist like you?" she asks gently.

"Yes, he was," I say. "He was extremely talented."

Will I tell her anything more or leave it at that? That sounds pretty innocent. Or will I tell her more of the serious stuff and trust I'll come out of it like her visitors, smiling and glad I shared?

"Would you like to tell me about him?" she asks.

"Oh," I say, completely unprepared for this question.

Marta continues to look at me with compassion. She's giving me her full attention. I'm still not sure I want to talk. I want to hear her story.

"The wine's really nice," I say. "I'm no wine buff, but this is lovely."

Marta smiles and refills our glasses. We drink in silence while I wait for intuition to guide me.

"My first husband was one of the most talented students at our art college," I tell her. "He won all the prizes, all the scholarships. He had his first exhibition when he was nine!" Marta looks surprised.

"He was a kind of child prodigy."

"Nine years old?"

We laugh. I hear noises in the garden. Somebody's coming to visit. I'm half relieved, but this sister or grandmother figure has managed to open an old memory door. It's hard to shut it while she's here beside me. The footsteps and voices disappear.

"I'd been in love with a poet," I tell her. "An artist, sculptor, philosopher, avant-guard poet who later became famous! But it didn't work out." I feel my body go numb. I hardly ever tell this story.

Marta smiles encouragingly.

"I met my first husband a year later. A friend of his waged a bet he wouldn't be able get me to go on a date with him." I have few memories to smile about with my first husband, but this is one.

Like deciphering a map, I study the back of my hands on my lap under Marta's table. I stare at the tanned skin, the knuckles that look like smiling mouths, the interesting lines sweeping from east to west. A few new aging spots look like star constellations. And there's the scar, still, thanks to big brother Andrew. Lost in navigating this information, a landslide of memories sweeps me back in time.

IT'S A MONTH BEFORE MY WEDDING. I'm almost twenty one. Father Roland will marry us at Roslin Chapel. It's 1966. The wise priest has asked us if we really, honestly think we can 'stick together till death do us part'. We're sitting in the shack of a dwelling which is his home. He's almost laughing as he asks the question. I'm thinking I'll give it my best, but I'm sure my young husband will find somebody else quickly, if I die. Four years later, two babies in tow, heart-broken, I'm back in Father Roland's sitting room and he's asking me to view my life as a movie. Rise above your physical body, he says, and look down on the drama.

Emma, Aram-Aitch and Andrew come to the wedding. Andrew's been appointed best man by somebody, not me. He and I get lost going to the chapel. We're deep in the country. The road is lined with hedges six feet high. The driver is stopping the car. He's mumbling "What now?" Andrew hardly ever talks, so I'm suggesting he gets out and helps the driver reverse into a field. Andrew opens the door and somehow manages to fall backwards into the mud. He's wearing a top hat and a hired wedding suit. His face turns scarlet.

My beautiful gold Kurt Geiger wedding shoes cost twice the price of my simple, white 1960's mini-wedding-dress. Aram-Aitch says to my husband "I hope you know what you're taking on young man!". Funny the things which stick in the mind.

"IT WAS HARD FOR ME being married," I tell Marta. "I didn't choose my husbands, they chose me. I know now that my greatest need in life is to be free. It's always been my coping mechanism and it got blocked. Marriage confused and caged me and my childhood wasn't a training ground for healthy relationships. I tried a few times to be married. My first marriage gave me my children. These are my priceless gifts in life. My best-ever creations. My masterpieces. Our masterpieces. Ah, if only they knew."

Marta nods, sips her wine and smiles. We sink into silence again while she allows me to remember more. I glance up at Alfonso on the dresser. It's almost like she's putting a spell on me.

"My second marriage gave me the opportunity to create my dream. My very own private art school," I tell her. "Very different from teaching art in schools which I'd done for twelve years. My second husband was an architect. He generously gave me part of his office, which was a converted warehouse beside the harbour, to start my own art school."

Marta's waiting for more information, yet she doesn't ask any questions.

"My dream for the school was born when I was seventeen, but didn't manifest until twenty three years later."

I pause to check what my body tells me about sharing how I become an artist, how my dream is born. My body feels calm.

"I left home when I was sixteen," I tell her. "I was deeply unhappy after years of verbal bullying and other unpleasant things. I packed a backpack and hitchhiked to Europe. I spent the next six months travelling from art gallery to art gallery. I explored Germany, Holland, Belgium and northern France. Some kind old gentleman left me fifty pounds in his will, so this financed my journey. My mission was to discover if I too could become an artist!"

I'm choosing now which bits of my story to withhold. Not because I don't want to share my story with her, but because my Spanish isn't good enough to paint a true picture. Silly really, because Marta's communication is ninety five per cent empathy, five per cent words.

MY HEART SKIPS BACK TO EUROPE. It's 1962. I'm seventeen. The new architecture I find in Germany is wildly exciting. I've never seen a town hall that's a massive silver dome on stilts, or an extraordinary art gallery that looks like a sculpture itself. My Edinburgh childhood is dominated by grand grey Georgian and neoclassical buildings and the scary Victorian Edinburgh Royal Infirmary: places for grown ups, not teenage-friendly. Here buildings are fun; they make you smile and sigh and blink. Buildings like the Berlin Philharmonic Hall, with its exuberant yellow exterior walls and its main roof shaped like a nomad's tent.

I meet young and old artists in communist East Berlin in a back street bookshop/meeting place. Many want me to help them escape. They explain their plans in detail. Over a period of two weeks, as requested, I smuggle in illegal Peter Stuyvesant cigarettes for them, in my boots and under my brown crocheted hat. They're grateful but they want more. They want out. They want help. There's a young woman called Clara who almost persuades me with the simplicity of her escape plan. I go to a cafe to think about it. Conscious I'm being followed by three men, I return to West Berlin for the night.

The terrifying severity and the unfairness of the Berlin Wall is overwhelming. There's constant shooting. Torches flash all night between the east and the west. Every day and every night desperate people attempt to escape. Crosses on both sides of the wall mark where they've failed. It's easy as a tourist to enter the East. It just requires a piece of paper at the checkpoint.

The following day, entering East Berlin supposedly to visit the national art gallery, I quickly realise I'm being followed again by the secret police. I keep well clear of Clara and the bookshop. There's a shooting incident on a piece of wasteland near the gallery, then five minutes later, a huge frightening mass of people, a political rally, surges and sweeps me up in its wake. I feel like a tiny leaf blown into the eye of a hurricane. I'm pushed, shoved, stared at, elbowed, and then knocked to the ground. It's obvious it's not safe to be here anymore, but I'm loath to abandon Clara, even though I know I cannot help her escape. Later the same day on my return to West Berlin, bruised and dirty, I'm arrested and taken off the metro at an unused unlit East Berlin underground station, and questioned for hours. After my release I move to Hamburg, find new friends, drift into

Amsterdam, discover flea markets and more bookshops and make more artist/writer friends. Then I find myself in Bruges and Lille, exploring Renaissance art and more inspiring architecture.

Throughout this journey I discover unforgettable buildings, haunting paintings, exciting sculptures and stories that send my imagination spiralling. Bookshops and chance encounters with fellow travellers along the way introduce me to the world of contemporary literature. I devour every book by Hermann Hesse I can lay hands on. I particularly love Eastern European, Russian and Chinese stories, so different from Burns and Blake and tales from Great Old Britain. I'm moved to the core by Jewish Isaac Beshevis Singer and I'm dazzled by Sartre, Camus, Jean Cocteau, Steinbeck and exile John Berger. Then there's Apollinaire, Rimbaud, Fernando Arrabal and a host of other extraordinary French, Spanish and German authors, playwrights-film-maker-poet-artists.

These artists and writers and thinkers become my family, though they don't know it of course. Their works feed my soul. Fiction and art become more interesting than real life. Role models slip into place from the strangest of scenarios.

Can I join these people? Can I too be an artist or a writer? Or both? Am I part of this tribe? Am I like them in any small way?

Poetry becomes a kind of internal guide for me, my wilderness guide, a decipherer of the ongoing confusion of what 'real life' is all about. One of my favourite poets is the Black American Langston Hughes:

> *Hold fast to dreams*
> *For if dreams die*
> *Life is a broken-winged bird*
> *That cannot fly.*

Hold fast to dreams
For when dreams go
Life is a barren field
Frozen with snow.

"I HAVE A MEETING at school now," Marta tells me, breaking the silence we've created. "But I'll be back in an hour. I want to hear about your dream. I had a dream too, once upon a time."

She glances around the room and I see her gaze perching on the photo of her handsome husband.

I watch her collect her bag, straighten her sweater and walk out into the chicken-filled garden. A few minutes after she leaves, I stand at the front door and observe her walking down the dirt track street. She walks purposefully. A small stocky frame encasing a tragedy and heart of gold.

Chapter 6

IT'S TWO HOURS LATER WHEN MARTA RETURNS. I've been busy having a shower with the tepid water. I'm now making some hot coffee in the kitchen; Marta joins me and surprises me by taking up the conversation exactly where we left off.

"So—your dream!" She smiles, sits down and accepts the coffee I offer her.

"Well," I say, not sure where to start.

We look each other straight in the eye.

"Well—well, when I returned to Scotland after my trip to Europe, I got a job in a chocolate factory. I needed money to become an artist!"

This now leads into the back story to how my dream is born. Do I really want to share it? Is Marta really interested and why is she interested?

"What about *your* dream?" I ask quietly.

"My dream?" she asks quickly.

"Yes, I'd love to know about your dream, your dreams."

"I don't dream any more. I used to dream. After Alfonso died—well, now I dream the best for my children and the children in our school of course."

"But—?" my questions feel intrusive. But what was your dream with Alfonso? I want to ask—and what about a dream for yourself now?

"There are no wants, no buts and no what-ifs in my life now, Margarita. I'd love to hear the story about your dream; I used to write too you know. Don't be shy, tell me."

It seems Marta has re-routed her dreams from herself to the next generation. It's not that her dreams have become a broken-winged bird; more like she's a wise, middle-aged owl encouraging love to unfold, all around her.

"So—?" she says.

"So, the chocolate factory was over a hundred years old. It was falling apart—dark, daunting and Dickensian—with wooden ladders leading to upper floors. I took the job because it was the only one that came my way."

Memories begin to fall like confetti all around my head.

MY NEW FRIEND SARA, the sexy, seventeen year old queen of Edinburgh's beatniks, found me the job. Aged sixteen, unhappy Sara ran away from her widowed father's house in Perth for the bright lights and LSD of bohemian Edinburgh, soon to be followed by her faithful sixty year old, diminutive nanny, Little Dear, accompanied by her small dog Pisser. Or was it Fyfer? Along with Sara's exotic brother Anthony, who was studying hallucinogenic drugs and anthropology simultaneously, the three lived in a tiny attic flat off Edinburgh's Royal Mile. Little Dear would become the catalyst for my second TV play in 1983, based on the discovery that RMH had joined a euthanasia organisation. The black comedy was called 'Exit Little Dear'.

"WE STARTED FILLING THE CHOCOLATE BOXES at five in the morning," I tell Marta.

"The conveyor belt was very fast! I was too slow. So I was put in a gloomy corner and told to wrap individual chocolates in gold and silver paper. This gave me the perfect opportunity to dream about all the paintings and sculptures I'd discovered, remember all the adventures I'd had along the way, and imagine my future as a fledgling artist."

Marta puts sugar in her coffee. Her spoon clinks on the side of the chipped cup. I pause, and our eyes meet. I'm at home with this woman in more ways than one.

Factory life was tough I remember. Many fights would break out daily between the women; I never understood what started them. It was especially dangerous leaving the factory. A lot of hair got pulled out, backsides kicked, faces slapped, scratched and bashed. Sara and I would run for the bus. At night I would go to drawing classes at the art college. My enthusiasm was boundless and the tutors tired, disinterested and discouraging.

"My adopted parents didn't support my choice to become an artist, so I lived with a Swedish friend whose father was a bookseller and whose mother was a witch!" Marta nods and laughs.

"We lived on porridge made overnight in a hay box, rice with mushroom stalks for supper and not much else, except chocolate. Five months later I went to London to learn to be an artist."

I glance again at Alfonso, wedged between two dusty dinner plates and a crystal vase. I wonder what his teenage years were like. Marta's phone rings. I'm left briefly to remember the next chapter of how I became an artist, despite the odds and how my dream was born.

AFTER FIVE MONTHS wrapping special chocolates, I earn enough money to go to London. I've read of a private art school where anybody can attend. 'Students' can either pay for tuition or rent an easel and a bit of floor space. I have enough money for the easel and the floor space, for six months. I'm hoping this will be time enough to discover if there is a real artist inside me, and if so, I'll apply to a proper art college where I can be taught.

*I arrive in London in 1962 after a blazing showdown with Aram-Aitch. For the first time in my life I find a voice for my anger. The racist bullying has gone on too long and has gone too far. Andrew, as ever, has nothing to say. I leave before I have to confront Emma. It's obvious I've become a serious disappointment to her, and she to me, although I don't realise this for about twenty five years. I have yet to discover that no parent, however idealistic and well meaning, is perfect. I've arrived at the point where I can do nothing right in my guardians' eyes. So I decide to take full responsibility for my young life and leave. If I don't leave now, right now, I **know** I'll become that broken-winged bird that will never ever fly.*

In one of the worst London fogs in living memory, I miraculously find my way to the art school, clutching my hard-earned factory money tightly in my hand. For the next six months I draw and paint every day. I've found paradise. My guardians reluctantly supply me with a small monthly cheque. When it runs out, I supplement it by making sandwiches for a football team on Saturday mornings and by modelling for real art students at the prestigious art schools in central London. The modelling provides large sums of money, four times the Saturday sandwich money, but comes at a price. I hate it more than words can say. It is a joy and an adventure for me to draw the naked body, but to have mine studied—for a secretive seventeen year old, it's a nightmare.

After my six months at the Heatherly School of Fine Art (the private art school), I decide I'm definitely an artist in the making. So I apply with a bulging portfolio of vibrant drawings and look-alike Fauve paintings to the real art schools in London and win a place at a few. I choose St Martins in central London, and soon discover my private art school was just kindergarten paradise. Now I've found Grown Up Heaven. I must be the keenest student they've ever had. London is exploding with youth culture. The Beatles have arrived, so has Pop Art from America. Ideas are everything. Soho, the hub of creative London, is just around the corner. Soho is a world full of exotic ladies of the night, bars where philosophers and writers meet and talk till dawn, bookshops, small cinemas, cheap Italian restaurants and artists carrying their paintings from studios to galleries. Our drawing models are all Soho ladies. Only occasionally now do I have to join them in the evenings, modelling at other art colleges, to pay for my rent. Emma is kindly, but reluctantly, funding me.

"SO THIS IS HOW my first dream was born," I tell Marta.

"I wanted to re-create the private art school which set me on my way to becoming an artist. I wanted to create a place where *anybody* who was passionate about drawing and painting could learn. I'm very grateful to my second husband for giving me this opportunity. The space he gave me adjoining his office was a perfect start for the classes. After a few years, when the marriage collapsed, I found another bigger warehouse, which was even better."

"Where was your art school?" Marta enquires.

"In Aberdeen, in Scotland."

"Did you teach children too?"

"Yes, children came on Saturday mornings. I love teaching children, I love children."

"Did you train as a teacher?"

"I did—yes I did. My sons were five and six when I returned to college. I taught in schools for twelve years. Then when I remarried, I got this chance to open my very own art school."

I remember my art school with joy. I called it the Independent Painters Workshop, IPW.

More confetti memories tumble down.

IT'S 1986. I'm forty one. I think I've found my real life's calling, encouraging other people to be creative. I feel I'm the luckiest person I know, work-wise. Health and home life are completely different matters.

Sixteen students enrol for the first term. My own art work, which has been dormant for seventeen years while I've been bringing up my children, springs to life and becomes rich, impulsive, intuitive and vibrant. I'm painting French farmers in beautiful French landscapes, children being cared for and exciting quick studies of nudes with large brushes, thick paint and vibrant pastels. I'm intoxicated with colour and daring to be bold. I'm unstoppable in my enthusiasm like every real artist I've ever read about.

I find a wonderful teaching colleague for my school called Rob, a graphic artist, with whom I learn, for the first time in my life, the meaning of co-creation. Rob's artwork is stunningly realistic, brilliantly planned, amazingly detailed and flawlessly executed. We admire each other's differences and create exciting courses together, including painting holidays and a popular course called Painting for the Terrified.

IT'S AMAZING HOW QUICKLY MEMORIES FLASH though the mind. We're still sitting at Marta's kitchen table, looking out through the open door into her garden. Our coffee in the old silver percolator is cold. The chocolate biscuits are all eaten. Her brown and white chickens are scavenging, unearthing titbits in the yard, the same way my mind keeps unearthing and feeding me insights about how I've come to be who I am today. Marta is a catalyst. No wonder her house is always full of people seeking help and understanding and love.

My memories shift. They're not like soft pretty confetti now. They're hard, uncomfortable, like the rice and coins people throw in place of confetti.

TEN YEARS AFTER opening my art school, one hundred and forty students are taking classes every week. I have a staff of three inspirational, professional artist teachers, including Mike, a gifted and charismatic early-retired army officer, a self-taught artist with a deep religious calling. He becomes a treasured friend. But despite the success, I close the school to take a year's sabbatical. Life events catch up with me. My second marriage collapses. Emma, my birth mother Lucie, my beloved partner and three close friends all die within eighteen months of each other. I lose my newly-found Christian faith which I thought would enable me to stay married whatever happened. Second time around, I'd promised God it would be for Life. I'm as devastated with God as I am with myself. If God is a loving father, what father would allow all this to happen to his beloved child? I know nothing about fatherly love. I can't begin to grasp the concept. It takes a while, many years, to see what a gift these bereavement experiences give me.

Slowly, slowly, I discover what faith means to me in the limitless sense of the word. I take the gender out of the Divine. I have to. I look around the world for other ways of understanding this 'phenomenon', Divine Love, and discover the teachings of Ram Dass and Andrew Harvey. Eventually, I find my own direct path to the mysterious place where the ego is silent and the heart is wide open to compassion. But I need my year's sabbatical to become seven years for this to happen. And I need to leave Scotland and live alone in the remote mountains of Spain and Alaska for this awakening to process. I need to become a nomadic artist. After years teaching and encouraging others how to access their true creativity, it's time to do it for myself.

My sons find my life change impossible to understand and I find it impossible to explain. I've lost my voice, but I've found my new path. The seven, silent, wilderness years become an archetypal journey, complete with all the archetypal characters at play—the shape shifter, the tricksters, the shadow, the allies and two extraordinary mentors, a French clown, Didier Danthois, and a Canadian artist/photographer/wilderness guide, Gernot Dick. But at the time, I don't see the bigger picture unfolding. I just know I have to find a meaning for all this heartbreak and gradually, though writing and drawing, silence and nature, prayer and meditation, it emerges.

Finally, I come down from my metaphorical mountain convinced there is a power greater than ourselves at work, that there is a bigger picture playing out for all our destinies, which is wonderful, loving and meaningful. The price for this realisation is the losing of my credibility with my sons. So now I am at peace with myself, but even more alone than ever.

MY HERMIT THOUGHTS come back into Marta's friendly kitchen. It's time for the chickens to roost.

"Do you still see your second husband?" she asks, getting up from the table.

"No," I say. "I don't."

"Is that okay?" She walks towards the door.

"Yes." I say.

"My two husbands had a hard time with me—and I with them."

I choose to stop the story at this point. I'm going to edit all the dark bits about the second marriage. I've said enough and I think she's heard enough.

Before Marta steps into the garden to round up her hens for the night, she invites me to visit her school tomorrow morning to meet the headmaster and visit some of the classrooms. I'm ecstatic.

Maybe this will be my story?

Widowed wife of daring pilot gunned down in Pinochet uprising, teacher in remote village school beside raging turquoise river, friend to the native population—

We're to meet in the school entrance hall after morning break.

"Come at eleven," she says, and disappears.

IT'S EARLY EVENING now and Alyssa, Jason and I sit down at Marta's square kitchen table. I seem to be living in the kitchen. The back door is now closed, it's getting chilly.

The chickens are safely in their shed. Marta's working on the computer. The kitchen's a small dark room with a large old fashioned stove. A black kettle hisses behind us. A tiny sink in a shadowy corner is chock-a-block with abandoned lunch dishes. Marta's youngest son, Juanito, home from a short vacation from University, is still outside repainting the house white.

We soak in Alyssa's stories as she munches peanuts and sips herbal tea.

"Chiloé," she says in answer to my question, "*the mystical island* the guidebooks all talk about, is flat, but surrounded by dramatic coastlines. Great if you like fishing or eating fresh fish. Then there are the weekly craft fairs. Wonderful woollen goods, hand-knitted by lots of locals. The knitwear is a very important source of income for many people. The island has seen some dire times; many emigrated south thirty, forty, eighty years ago, because life was too hard there. The government gave away free land in the south up to twenty years ago to encourage settlements down there, so many islanders sailed to Tortel. That's where a hundred or so died in mysterious circumstances."

"What happened?" I ask, knowing some of the stories.

Alyssa shrugs her shoulders.

"Dunno," she says. "No idea."

"What about the ferry from Chaiten to the south?" I ask. "Have you any news about it?"

I'm overly excited about catching this ferry. Travelling slowly by sea has a special fascination.

"Yes—no," Alyssa continues. "There are two ferries going south but one sank last week. Well almost sank. It's chaos now because everybody wants to go on the other one, that's all I know."

"And Chaiten, is it a town? What's it like?"

"Chaiten is a small important ferry and catamaran port. It's also the Casa Redonda, the roundhouse and it's Gabor and Andres." She looks at us and smiles.

She has a story here, I can feel it coming.

WE SIT SPELLBOUND as Alyssa describes Gabor's wooden roundhouse hostal which he has built himself, around a tree. He's just finished building it. It's right beside a river with spectacular panoramic views of the volcano and the exotic Rio Blanco valley with its forested mountains disappearing into the clouds.

"The view's a bit like a Japanese print on a misty day," Alyssa tells us. "This is rainforest country. Lots of rain there all the time. Casa Redonda is just a stone's throw from the fabulous Pumalín Park which was bought by an American billionaire not so long ago."

"Gabor," Alyssa continues, "is a musical genius, a serious classical guitar concert performer, an expert fly-fisherman, an origami master, an artist, an art collector. And now he's built a hostal for world travellers. But—" Her pretty face winces.

"He's got one terrible personality flaw. He has appalling mood swings, much worse than any woman I know! He screamed at me for using the cooker before he'd finished cooking his own supper! He started swearing at me in English then German. All because I boiled some water while he was frying his bl**dy hamburgers!"

We commiserate with surprised looks.

"So I spent the next morning in the cyber café," she said. "I just felt so awful."

There follows a long pause.

"And Andres?" I ask. "Who is he?"

"Oh, Andres!" sighs Alyssa. Her face radiates a huge smile.

"Very different from Gabor. Andres is a wonderful, gentle, fascinating soul. A Canadian with a mysterious past. He's very secretive about his past. He's a wilderness guide who loves music. He'll play his *charango*—that's a small instrument like a cross between a ukulele, a banjo and a guitar—anywhere—in the rainforest, on the black beach at sundown, by the lagoon in the high mountains, anywhere he feels like it. When he doesn't need to walk or talk or guide, he just sits down and plays and sometimes he sings. He sings beautifully."

LATER, I chat again with Marta.

"Do you know Gabor and Andres?" I ask her.

"Gabor—no. Andres—of course. Everybody knows Andres. He's a kayak and rafting guide, a Canadian, a lovely, gentle person; he often brings people to Futaleufú to fish or raft or hike. Yes, he stays here too."

I'm one hundred per cent intrigued. The magic ingredients are all here: Canadian, wilderness guide, explorer, mystery, music, gentleness. I feel myself falling in love with the legend way before meeting the man.

EARLY THE NEXT MORNING, before my visit to the newly rebuilt primary school, I explore the village. I feel an excitement here I'd hoped to find in El Bolsón. Futa is a small, compact community. Plump chickens run around outside ramshackle wooden houses, sheep are tethered beside front doors. Most of the houses are old, about forty or fifty years old, at a guess. Each house is unique; every house is made of wood. Some are painted, some stained. No alpine-style kit-cabins here. Outside the few shops, horses are left grazing while their owners stock up. The shops are often a front room of somebody's home. Each shop seems to sell roughly the same items—a small selection of fruit, a few vegetables. Change is given in shops in the form of a handful of sweeties. Ox-carts pull newly-felled tree trunks. No road is paved, everywhere is a dirt track road leading to a life I want to find out about.

Surrounding Futaleufú, wilderness stretches out for hundreds of miles. I remember the satellite photo of the Prussian-blue lakes and the snow-dusted mountains. The beauty of the place is truly humbling. The two raging turquoise rivers, the Futa and the Azul, hurtle their way though gorges, thrust past sandy beaches with deep, frothing pools, pound massive boulders over miles of incredibly dangerous rapids and eventually merge with the sea at Chaiten. At some point they join. I can't begin to imagine the kind of courage people must have to want to play on these waters.

I have a growing feeling things are about to unfold here. That's when I meet Lorinda.

Chapter 7

By law, restaurants in Chile have to serve cheaper, fixed-price meals at lunch time. In Argentina, budget travellers can try the *tenedor libre*—'free fork'—restaurants where you can eat all you want for a fixed price.

LORINDA is the owner of a charming, quaint, wooden café-cum-craft shop-art gallery. Lorinda is small, slim, brown-haired, tactile, about fifty five. She tells me Futa has only been accessible by road since 1982, that Futaleufú means *big river* in the Mapuche language. She explains there are many indigenous families living around here; they are mostly farmers and loggers. They're very poor, she tells me. There's a beautiful magical glacial lake nearby. She talks about magic and synchronicity a lot. Above her craft shop there's an apartment she lets to visitors, she gives me a guided tour.

Downstairs in the café once again, Lorinda disappears into the kitchen to make me a fruit juice with local strawberries and pears. She makes herself a tea with fresh herbs, explaining the medical qualities of each leaf, and we talk like long-lost sisters. She asks if I'd like to rent the upstairs rooms. I explain I'm looking for somewhere to come back to next winter, and maybe, just maybe, it could be here. She asks me if I'd like to come back to the café for supper, and describes what she's planning to cook. I ask if she'd like two more customers. Jason and Alyssa might like to come. I explain if they been successful fishing, we'll be having fish for supper. Lorinda laughs. We part smiling, hearts singing.

AT ELEVEN O'CLOCK, I arrive at the village school to meet Marta and the headmaster. Rain pours down. My newly bought purple rain-jacket is not sufficient for this kind of deluge. I'm actually wetter inside the jacket than outside. In the headmaster's office I try elegantly to shed the dripping garment. It's a tricky manoeuvre. Middle-aged Señor Gomez kindly ignores the pools of water sliding under his desk. He listens carefully to Marta's summary of my life.

"Irish artist—for many years teacher of art to children and adults—created her own art school in Scotland. Retired from teaching now but has a retreat house in a mountain village in Spain where she offers spiritual and creative retreats. Two sons, and a grandmother to two little girls and one baby boy. She's brought some of her artwork to show us."

The headmaster smiles.

"Show me," he says quietly.

I hand him the colourful collection of my oil and acrylic paintings, photocopied and reproduced as art cards. The cards are small and easy to handle.

Many of the images are of children from around the world, some are praying. Señor Gomez scrutinises each card then passes it slowly to Marta. The first image he examines is a tender, cadmium yellow and Prussian blue illustration from a Lebanese folk tale called Zoshie and the Shepherd. The young shepherd has had a spell put on him by a wicked witch and Zoshie, his six year old only friend, pledges to search the world to find an antidote.

Before studying the next cards, the busy headmaster moves his head from side to side, as though exercising his neck muscles. He examines with concentration a collection of multi-coloured clown drawings and paintings inspired by my first spiritual teacher, Didier Danthois, a Buddhist/clown.

I watch a small smile soften the Argentinean's face as he looks at the turquoise image portraying a beautiful Persian woman, a timeless symbol of the Muslim faith.

I've also included a card of a painting of two brave, young prayerful monks who lived on the lonely Skellig Michael Rock, twelve miles off the coast of County Kerry in Ireland in the fifth century; 'living their lives, celebrating their faith on the margin, on the edge of the world'. This image and the remoteness of their community, along with the drawings of two ancient Inuits, also living their lives in the remotest of places, have haunted me for years. It's a new phenomenon for me to love the images I create. Amazing how self-criticism can turn to humble appreciation.

The headmaster handles and examines each card as if it were a fragile, rare bird's egg. He lingers over the vibrant digital drawing of my Jewish father Lionel. I'm never going to be able to meet or find out the real truth about my dad, so a few years back I decided to invent him, and give him a name, Lionel Rabinowitz. In the painting, he's a young Jewish refugee from Poland. He's sitting on a park bench in St. Stephen's Green in Dublin, busking, playing his violin, illuminated by a beautiful inner light—shining—despite everything.

The two teachers scan the remaining cards. There are many images of children expressing moments of deep compassion with damaged sea birds, moments of fear and forgiveness with betrayers. My paintings nowadays seem to be all about 'moments' of this or that. Mainly moments when a life changes for ever.

During the following minutes I feel connected to these two strangers through my paintings in a strange inexplicable way. I think this is what success means to me: when my images seem to touch people deeply. I feel a sense of completion and purpose. I feel happy. I feel successful! As they study each card carefully, I remember that these people are busy people, so I cut my commentary to the barest minimum. In fact, I say nothing.

Marta takes me on a tour of the school. I'm shocked to find the library has hardly any books. My mind spins, and I'm writing and publishing and selling children's books and donating all the profits to this school to buy reference and picture books for the children.

Could this be my story?

No. Not enough characters; not enough sub-themes.

But what about Marta's secret? What about her dream, her story, her writing?

What if I could unearth this story?

She's a closed book in many ways, and I respect her privacy. I think she's even more private than me!

In every class we visit, the teacher instructs the children to get up and greet me in the traditional fashion.

"Good morning, Aunty Margarita," they all say in unison, and grin.

When the children reach the age of eleven, they leave for boarding school in Chaiten, six hours away by bus from the village. When they go to university, they have to travel much further, to Puerto Montt or Valdiva. It's very hard on the young children. The parents often feel bereft. Some mothers can hardly bear this separation. One of Marta's great skills, it seems, is helping parents come to terms with this grief. This is one reason why her house is always full of people. Marta's an unofficial grief counsellor.

IN FUTALEUFÚ—which I still can't pronounce—I feel my journey has begun. There's something about this place which encapsulates much of what I'm searching for. There's the incredible beauty and the simplicity of the place, the fabulous turquoise rushing rivers, mountains all around and old, old trees. There's Lorinda's café-cum-meeting place. And there's Marta, an ambassadress of compassion and a real Samaritan in action.

Already I've gained some insights into the community. Lorinda tells me village life is like ripples on a pond, there are circles within circles of people here, and unless you live here all year round, and she doesn't, you never get to be part of the inner circle.

"Look at this painting," she said during one of our chats. "This artist had to leave because she was so disliked here, too different. But in the end she was selling her work to galleries in New York."

I study the large, confident, abstract image and wonder what was so different about her. There are no clues in the painting.

"What kind of paintings do you do?" Lorinda asks.

"Well, that's a difficult question to answer," I say. "Because my paintings don't translate very well into words."

"Are they abstract, or landscape, or—?"

Lorinda has a collection of small art works for sale in her gallery-craft shop. She has interesting taste and all her paintings appeal to my eye.

"What I usually say is my paintings are metaphysical, there's something behind the image, or there are many layers of images. I usually give people my website and say its best if they have a look for themselves".

"Do you use oils or acrylics?" she asks.

"I use everything, depending on where I am when I'm painting."

"Are you painting on this trip?"

"No, I'm story gathering! It takes a huge amount of energy for me to paint, I need time to prepare, time to be with the painting, and time afterwards to recover!"

"Recover! What do you mean, recover?"

We both laugh because it sounds ridiculous. Lorinda and I have already had many conversations where we've discovered we're both fascinated by the bigger picture of our individual and collective lives. We're both deeply interested in spirituality, but neither of us practises a religion as such, although I've twice been elected cleaner for the year for our village church and I love going to mass with my neighbours. We're usually about a congregation of ten. One hundred and ten when somebody dies.

I paint a word picture for Lorinda of the spiritual life of my Spanish village. It starts with the church cleaning ritual.

"When I wash the pews and sweep the old tiled floor I feel like a spiritual Cinderella," I tell her. "Because they're never, ever going to let me take communion and I'd love to. Every second Friday, I keep quiet and I keep cleaning while my lovely three co-cleaners change the flowers and dust St Anton with his broken finger, which I sort of repaired last summer. My cleaning friends replace the altar cloth, dust the confessional and talk about their families. I can't participate in these conversations because they're too local, too tied up with each others' family business."

I tell Lorinda how I overhear new words during these cleaning rituals, how I store them along with hundreds of other unused Spanish words in my head, how I wish my brain would release these captives more easily, but it doesn't. So I'm the semi-mute, Cinderella foreigner, who's not very good at cleaning or mending or communicating. But somehow it doesn't matter at all. Mass happens anyway.

We pause. Lorinda goes into the kitchen and returns with a plate of home-made cookies.

"Eat, Cinderella," she says, and we both laugh.

"Our church was once upon a time a mosque," I tell her.

"Village life in Andalucía is rich with quasi-religious rituals and ceremonies, all year round," I continue.

Outside in the street a man gallops past on his horse. My train of thought is interrupted.

"Where's he off to?" I ask.

"Probably to the bus depot."

"The bus depot?"

"To collect a parcel from the bus. So—the religious ceremonies in your village?"

"Well, we have Palm Sunday with a blessing, not of palms but olive branches, beside the local water trough. Corpus Christi is when the women make outdoor altars in front of their homes, covering the ground with rose petals and yellow gorse. I make one as well. Then in the evening, the whole village processes around the village singing and the priest kneels in front of each altar and blesses it."

Then there's an ancient candle ceremony in winter when the men light a bonfire outside the church door and we stand around it, in a circle, lighting our candles from the priest's, who lights his from the fire.

It touches me deeply to be with people who love the Divine in any form. Lorinda and I have both had many experiences when fate simply can't be called fate, when it seems an unseen hand guides, or a messenger comes right at the crucial moment and we turn left when we could have turned right. Left being where we meet gold, right being where we meet trouble. And we both agree that when the shit hits the fan, there's always an important lesson to learn, usually our most important lesson in fact.

Lorinda is in a questioning mood. She switches the conversation back to painting.

"So you recover from painting! What does that mean? Do you have to recover from writing too?!"

"No! Writing is different in some ways, but similar in others."

My new friend offers more of her home made coconut cookies.

"Finish them," she says. "And explain!"

Whenever we sit down to talk, the café is empty. Whenever we stop talking, people appear. The man on horseback passes the window again, this time with a large parcel balancing precariously on the saddle in front of him. The horse's bridle is made of pleated rope. Excited dogs run ahead, barking.

"So—?"

"So, what happens when I paint nowadays is that it's a whole process that I get lost in. It's not like choosing an interesting view, setting up your easel, maybe battling with weather conditions, then coming home with an atmospheric landscape. That's what most of my students wanted to learn to paint. They wanted to paint what they saw. I want to paint what happens after what I see settles. The way I make my paintings now is to put myself in landscapes whose energy stirs something very deep inside in me. Alaska does this, so does Patagonia. I absorb the colours, I sort of tune into the energy of the place, I can't really explain this in words. It's something like ... before, I would remember views by sketching them, now I remember a place by what I've sensed or connected with in my whole being, in my soul. That's why I call my paintings metaphysical. I'm trying to recreate something way beyond what I've seen and heard and felt. And I need to recover after making a painting because when I start to paint, it's an incredibly physical experience!"

Lorinda looks surprised and interested. Most of her paintings for sale are miniatures.

"What do you do exactly?"

"I start by texturing large surfaces with gesso. This means I'm slapping on thick layers of white paste then vigorously scraping it off and on and off again with all sorts of bits and pieces – wood, shells, cardboard, my hands, serrated knives. Each 'tool' leaves its unique pattern. I may imbed textures, string or tissue paper. When that's dry, I'll start intuitively painting layers upon layers of colour. I'll wipe lots off, repaint and wipe off again. Depending on which country I'm in, my colours will be either mainly blues, or browns, sometimes yellow. I did a series of yellow paintings in Canada a few years ago. The colours reflect for me the essence of the country, the feeling behind what I see. Once these two stages have been completed, that's when I disappear!"

"Disappear?" We laugh again. And however silly or odd this might sound, I know this is exactly what happens.

"Yes, I 'disappear' into the colours and textures of the images to find half-hidden clues. I become like an artist/detective, in a kind of a trance. You could say the soul whispers, it invites me in. Maybe there's a face, or a group of bodies, or an animal or a cave. There are always suggestions in the textures so I 'disappear' to find them, and then I accentuate them. Or, I'll start painting around something I find, and keep going until something completely new arrives."

Lorinda blinks. Am I losing her?

"You know when you meditate, you go some where else. I mean, when you get so into the meditation, you sort of leave your body and you just are, you are just Being, not Doing anything. You are just your spirit, unaware of your body. The same thing happens when people pray or listen to beautiful music I think. There comes a point where you are part of the music, or you are the prayer. You're drawn into a different space and a different sense of time. Out of your body, you're free and open to—open to what? Well, in painting, I'm open to creating whatever comes through me in this altered state."

I write down the name of my website. Lorinda remains silent.

"I need to recover when I do this kind of painting because it's so hard to come back from that altered state. It's impossible to have a normal conversation for hours. Impossible to do anything practical for hours. I need to sleep and be by myself for as long as it takes. I feel extremely vulnerable when I'm like this." We look at each other intently. Does she understand I wonder? Yes, I think she knows exactly what I'm talking about.

"It's called 'letting go and letting God' by some people. I call it taking the ego out of my art, allowing the most mysterious process imaginable to take place."

Lorinda looks at the card I've given her and smiles.

"That's a digital image," I tell her. "I photo a painting or a sketch, then transfer it to my computer. This process doesn't involve the same physical energy as painting, but I'll go deep into the same altered state. I'll play with the colours and shapes of the painting until the alchemy works, and a completely new image springs into being. I'm always amazed at what appears. It's real magic!"

And that's how my writing unfolds, I tell her. After the story 'gathering' is complete, music, or sometimes silence, lead me into an altered state, where words will write themselves and all I have to do is allow the process to happen. That's what happened when I wrote my TV plays. It was as easy and natural as a candle surrendering to its own flame. Then I spend months crafting the writing. Rewriting. Adding and subtracting. Shaping and sharpening. Expanding and reducing. Then the alchemy starts all over again. Lorinda smiles. We sit in comfortable silence for a long time.

Then two men arrive and ask for sandwiches.

AROUND SEVEN O'CLOCK on day two in Futa, after my school visit and two more fruit drinks at Lorinda's, Jason and Alyssa return from the fishing expedition with the husband of Marta's friend.

"I just invited myself along," beams Alyssa. "Always wanted to learn how to fly-fish, so I reckoned Jason was my man. Look what he caught!"

Jason's inner light is ignited. He's a happy man again. The expedition was a great success. Then the pantomime which is called preparing the trout for supper begins. By eleven o'clock it is almost ready to be accompanied by potatoes dug up especially from Marta's garden. Effortlessly, we get through four bottles of local wine during the time it takes to prepare the meal.

Tomorrow Jason will catch the famous 6.30 a.m. bus to Chaiten. His next adventure will be the eight-seater plane back to Puerto Montt.

"Are you going back to visit the German girls in Puerto Veras?" I ask as he finishes the remains of his rainbow trout.

"No!" he says. "No, no no!"

We laugh, enjoying a moment of a brief, shared past.

THE LAST EVENING with Jason is full of the wonderful *something* travellers create amongst themselves. It's a kind of instant bonding. We're interested in the same things; there are stories and information to share generously. We feel part of the same travelling tribe, connected by our separateness. We need each other's company for a short while. I think we're all being *drawn by our star.*

We've been joined by Julie, another young German girl, a gentle, studious soul who's just arrived from Chaiten. She also stayed at Casa Redonda. She tells us her stories about Gabor and Andres.

"Ah, Andres," she sighs, just as Alyssa had sighed.

"He's lovely. We went on an amazing trek with him to a lagoon. We didn't get home till about nine thirty, what a day. First we drove around Chaiten buying picnic supplies, 'Best bread here,' he would say, 'best empanadas there, German cakes here and melons over there.' Everybody stocked up as if we were going away for a month. All the shopkeepers greeted Andres like he was their favourite son, a favourite uncle, their dad, or their best friend. He played his banjo/ukulele many times. He's so knowledgeable about all the wildlife and trees. There are trees near Chaiten which are three thousand years old. We saw them. They're absolutely incredible."

'PURPLE ANGEL' ACRYLIC ON PAPER

'MOMENT OF COMPASSION' PENCIL SKETCH

'INUIT WOMAN' GRAPHITE AND ACRYLIC ON PAPER

'SKELLIGMICHAEL MONKS' ACRYLIC ON CANVAS

Chapter 8

TWO DAYS LATER at 6.30 a.m. it's my turn to take the small, twelve-seater bus bound for Chaiten, Casa Redonda and the charismatic Andres, who has already unknowingly opened a heavy, creaky door right into my heart.

Could this be the story? I don't want it to be. I'm looking for somebody else's story. I'm choosing to be the witness, not the protagonist. I want to be the narrator at this point. But my heart is engaged. And what about the crisis? Is there a link here? What's going to happen now?

The scenery we pass is so beautiful I get neck-ache looking out of both windows. This section of the journey runs through long stretches of virgin rainforest, passing small villages, the white waters of Largo Yelcho and the Parque Nacional Queulat with its glaciers and waterfalls. We stop for breakfast at a village shack beside a muddy crossroads. About six of us, all locals except me, pile out of the bus and file into a tiny wooden shed which is the local café. Three tables are set and prepared for the bus travellers' breakfast. There's a pot of home-made jam, orangey coloured, a basket full of bread, a dish of butter, mugs, teaspoons, sugar and a jar of chocolate. The bread is more like a cross between a croissant and a freshly fried fritter with nothing in it. The way to eat it is to dunk the fritter in your steaming hot chocolate or coffee, and suck! It is sublimely delicious. Yet everybody else seems to be slurping and chewing and gazing into space. I feel like I have just discovered a world secret.

CHAITEN is built on the same grid system as Futaleufú. It's bigger and the grass-edged, dirt roads, which are wider, are full of chickens scavenging and horses grazing. Here, too, sheep are tied up in front gardens. A few houses have fences for this reason. This small harbour town is the capital of the province. It's surrounded by forest-clad hills and lies at the top of a quiet inlet which leads out into the Patagonia channels. For me, it's the springboard to the mysterious far south.

People seem to go about their business slowly here. I notice lots of young brown faces, schoolboys and girls wearing dark red uniforms. I forgot to ask Alyssa for directions to the Round House, so I seem to be going round the same block repeatedly. Finally I find my way.

"The hostal's close to the prison," somebody tells me.

As I approach the gaol, which is close to the river, I see a horse tethered outside. It's a wonderful little visual joke. A getaway horse, ready and waiting. Later I discover sheep-stealing is the main crime here.

CASA REDONDA IS ENCHANTING. It's wonderful. It's everything Alyssa and Julie have said – and more. It's a real oasis of peace, comfort and simplicity. Two extremely efficient young German girls are running the hostal. Gabor apparently has taken to spending most of the day in the loft with his new German girlfriend.

"*Very young* girlfriend," Alyssa had observed.

My room overlooks the river and the mist-shrouded mountains in the Pumalín National Park. There's art on every wall. A huge tree grows up through the communal area and a spiral staircase has been constructed around it. Circling its roots is an area of polished river stones. The minimal furniture is made of pine and everything else seems to be either Windsor blue or matt white. Everything is tasteful, unpretentious and new. There's been incredible attention to detail. All the traveller's needs have been considered. I discover later this is because Gabor himself has been a traveller for many years. He's travelled up and down the thousand kilometre Carretera Austral for the last ten years, fishing practically all its rivers.

Gabor explains to me that the paintings are a legacy from a friend of his who died a few years ago. There's some excellent work here: 1960s post-expressionist pen and ink drawings, lino prints and watercolours, all with a severe and strongly masculine orientation. This is the work of a serious artist intensely studying his personal world. Nothing happens by chance in his work. Everything feels inspired by his passion to examine the evidence. Gabor gives me a brief tour of the art collection and then points me in the direction of the ferry office.

At the ferry office I am not so much greeted with helpful information, as quickly ushered out as a complete a waste of time. Now that's a bit of an exaggeration, which perfectly explains my frustration at being misunderstood—and misunderstanding how the system works here. There is a ferry south, I'm told, but not for tourists—only for locals. Coming back, tourists can use the ferry, but not going down.

"No, you can't book for coming back. We don't yet know if the ferry will come back on that date, it's being repaired at the moment."

"I know," I say. "But what about the other ferry that is running?"

Once again I don't understand the answer to this question.

Maybe a bigger plan is unfolding for me which doesn't include a ferry on possibly treacherous waters. Or maybe after Tortel, I could go further south to Tierra del Fuego by boat. From there, there's a four day ferry back to Puerto Montt. I leave the ferry office with a sense of resignation, but with a real insight into how I have to learn to be more open to going with the flow here, more available to be drawn by my star.

Tourist? I'm not a tourist. I'm looking for a story. I'm a researcher!

BACK AT THE ROUND HOUSE, I meet twenty six year old Sylvie and twenty seven year old Raphael, from France. They're taking a year out from their jobs to travel around the world. Starting in Asia, they then moved on to explore Australia and New Zealand. Now they're beginning their South American adventure. We like each other immediately. Sylvie is calm, intelligent and beautiful with fine, long, blond hair. She looks German with her two pigtails pinned together at the top of her head. Raphael is smaller, handsome, dark-haired and speaks good Spanish. He's funny, witty and lively. He's an excellent photographer, Sylvie tells me. Like me, Raphael was educated at a Rudolf Steiner school. His parents grow organic vegetables somewhere near Lyon. Sylvie works in a government office, something to do with school administration. She doesn't talk about her family. The couple are heading south too, having just arrived by ferry from the mystical island of Chiloé.

They tell me how difficult it was to get information about the ferry and that the head office in Santiago was no help at all. Finally they heard a rumour a ferry was leaving at midnight.

"It was a great experience," Sylvie tells me. "But we didn't get much sleep. We just had reclining chairs for the ten hour night crossing."

They look at each other and grin.

I tell them about my attempts to get a ferry south. They commiserate.

"You'll either have to fly or go by road," they say.

"We're going south on the Carretera Austral."

It's one thousand kilometres of dirt track going right down the spine of Chile. I've read that stretches of this legendary, pebbled highway are punctuated by occasional small towns, remote settlements and isolated homesteads. Fleets of minibuses ferry passengers from the north to the south and back again. The timetables are said to be erratic. The buses often break down.

"You'll love it," Sylvie assures me when we swap more information.

"We're heading for Puyuhuapi, then Cochrane, then the very far south," she says.

Puyuhuapi—as unpronounceable as Futaleufú—is a tiny village at the top of a fjord where four brave and rich German explorers created a settlement in 1935. Hitler's chauffeur is rumoured to have lived there after the war. Sylvie gives me all their research in an excited outpouring. My new friends have certainly done their homework on this vast wilderness at the bottom of the globe, this land of sparkling lakes and smoking volcanoes, these thousand kilometres of solitude on a road leading to the majestic ice fields of the south.

"The daughter of one of the original pioneers still lives in the village in the red painted, wooden house her dad built." Sylvie is unstoppable with interesting information.

"It sounds wonderful," I say. Once again, I'm one hundred per cent hooked.

I tell them about Andres's famous hikes, nothing more and we decide to check him out tomorrow morning, together.

Chapter 9

Chile is one of South America's most stable and prosperous nations. It's been relatively free of the coups and arbitrary governments that have blighted the continent. The exception was the seventeen year rule of General Augusto Pinochet, whose 1973 coup was one of the bloodiest in twentieth century Latin America and whose dictatorship left more than three thousand people dead and missing. I've heard this number is wildly inaccurate. Many people met their death being pushed out of planes, a popular form of execution. There were, I have read, other forms of unspeakable and unimaginable cruelty.

THE NEXT MORNING I set off in the drizzle to find Andres's 'office'. Just outside the long, low, wooden hut which is his centre of operations, I meet Sylvie and Raphael as arranged. It's ten o'clock. They've discovered the cyber café and the bakery. Then, moments later, I'm standing in front of the legend.

Raphael asks Andres about tomorrow's hike into the Pumalín Park. A soft Canadian voice pours out a quiet avalanche of information. I stand behind the young couple and stare. He's medium height, looks a bit like a Cornish fisherman, wears dark blue corduroy trousers, a blue fleece and gumboots. His curly, grey, shoulder-length hair springs out from under a black, woolly, knitted hat. His face is beautiful, kind and watchful.

"So you'd like to do the hike tomorrow to Pumalín Park?" he asks. "You speak English?"

We nod.

"Well, the Park's a very special place. It's one of the most important conservation projects in the world." Andres pauses and looks for a reaction. Nobody challenges him.

"It's been created by the American billionaire Douglas Tompkins. Tompkins lives here for part of each year with his family. It's a private reserve extending over eight hundred thousand acres."

That's sixty miles of virgin wilderness from north to south, and between thirty and forty miles from the Pacific Ocean to the Argentina border. Vast. It's the largest of thirteen similar parks Tompkins has created in Chile and Argentina.

What sort of a person would buy—*could buy*—eight hundred thousand acres of virgin forest, I ask myself? And more. Months later I discover Mr Tompkins made his millions, a lot of them, in San Francisco as the founder of the North Face adventure and travel gear company. Most of Pumalín Park was purchased from one hundred and fifty heirs of a Spanish conquistador who deeded the land almost five hundred years ago.

"When the 'park' was first bought," Andres informs us, "it caused a lot of controversy, especially among the Chilean armed forces. But now the park has nature sanctuary status and that's calmed everything down."

Andres makes me feel I'm the first person ever to receive this information—how strange—his voice is hypnotic.

"The park covers large areas of the western Andes. Most of it is temperate rain forest. The aim of the project is to protect the lifestyles of all its inhabitants as well as protecting the physical environment. Tompkins has established a native tree nursery, producing one hundred thousand saplings of endangered species. He's also developed apiculture: in 2002 the Pumalín bee stations produced thirty thousand kilograms of honey."

The gentle Canadian stops for a brief second and smiles at Raphael and Sylvie.

"There are—"

"That's *a lot* of honey," interrupts Sylvie with her lovely French accent.

Andres agrees and then continues.

"There are treks ranging from short trails into the rainforest, to arduous hikes lasting a few days. There are three marked tracks leading to the Cascadas Escondidas, where you can see a three thousand year old alerce tree. Other treks to the lakes take longer."

He scans our faces, taking the group pulse. We're entranced. Well, I certainly am.

"One trek starts very early morning. It's the long hike to the Laguna Tronador."

This is the one Julie took.

"Up to ten different species of trees grow side by side up there."

He pauses to rearrange his woolly hat.

"There are many possibilities for hikes," concludes Andres. "Time, weather and fitness are all considerations."

"You want to come too?" He asks me, his brown eyes finding mine behind my drizzle-drenched glasses.

"Yes," I say.

"Names then, please," he asks. Sylvie and Raf comply.

"Meg Robinson," he says. "Irish." He studies my passport. You need to give passport numbers for almost everything in Chile it seems.

"Irish," he says again. "Meg Robinson ... " Then he fixes me with a charming smile and tries to find a word.

I smile, he smiles—the words don't arrive. Then—some gobbledegook—

"*Cad á mara tá tú?* That's the Irish greeting," he says. "Gaelic for *how are you?* You don't know it?" He looks mystified.

"Maybe it's my accent." He tries again. I smile, he smiles. "No—sorry—I don't speak Irish," I say.

"That's because I was born in Ireland but brought up in Scotland, adopted," I explain. I don't know why I give him this bit of personal info. "Yes, adopted, so I'm Irish but I know more about Scotland."

"Do you speak Scottish Gaelic?" he asks, as we seem to wipe out the fact there are two other people waiting for tickets or confirmation that we really are going tomorrow. Time stands still and I feel I'm being involuntarily drawn into a story.

"Are you coming to play music at the hostal tonight?" I ask as we leave. "I hear you do sometimes."

"No," he says. "Well, maybe. I don't know yet. We'll see. Possibly. See you all tomorrow anyway at ten o'clock. Come at ten."

THE NEXT MORNING it's raining hard. A young German kayaker has joined us at the Round House. He's keen to do the hike so we head off together at a quarter to ten. At ten o'clock there's no sign of anybody outside Andres's wooden office. At a quarter past ten he arrives wearing the same woolly fisherman's hat he had on yesterday and tells us it's somebody's birthday, so the boy who should have opened the office hasn't turned up and there's a problem with a lorry going to Futaleufú. He's going to have to drive it there himself. But never mind, he says, I've got a friend to take you on the hike. A local man.

"Does he speak English?" Sylvie asks.

"Yes," replies Andres with a grin. "He says 'yes' and 'no'!"

I'm wondering why his friend can't drive the lorry and Andres take us as arranged. I feel silenced by an overwhelming sense of disappointment. After all the stories about him, all that anticipation, the day in the rain forest with *the legend* isn't going to happen. How could this be? I want to leave now; I don't want to have these kinds of feelings. But I can't leave, or rather I feel I can't, because they need four people to make the trek happen.

MARCUS, AGED ABOUT sixty, Andres's replacement, turns up at 10.45 a.m. He wears thick dark framed glasses, a black, slightly shinny raincoat over a white shirt, a sombre tie, grey striped, trousers, and well-worn white trainers. He's also wearing a small baseball cap. His outdoor gear doesn't match my picture of a wilderness guide.

We set off in the minibus to do the picnic shopping. Best bread in town here, best empanadas (Chilean pasties) there, best German cakes, water—

"¿Todo bien?" he enquires—everybody okay, everything okay? He's chirpy. He grins a lot. It's true, Marcus doesn't appear to speak any more English than "yes" or "no", so I get the job of group translator. Later we discover he has a few other words in his repertoire.

"Dheese beeeg tree – dheeese babee tree – beeeg tree zree zousand years old. Babee tree one undred!"

It's going to be a two hour drive into the Pumalín Park, then two hikes; one could be two hours the other shorter.

Then at sunset we'll end up on Santa Barbara beach, where there are said to be hundreds of dolphins playing close to the shore. The beach is black, volcanic sand peppered with silver shells.

DURING THE TWO HOUR DRIVE into the park, the rain pours down. We stop to see a wayside hot spring which Marcus's cousin cunningly found after many years of searching. Ingeniously they finally decided to hunt for it in winter, when the hot steam would be visible from the roadside. Clever tactic.

"Andres doesn't know about this hot spring," boasts our guide with a wide grin.

I bet he does, I say to myself.

Marcus is a grandfather, so we swap grandchildren notes. He is medium height, has short dark bushy hair, drives carefully and, although he doesn't look at all an outdoors sort of person, nor does he have Andres's famous musical talent, he turns out to be an angel in disguise.

At the start of our first hike into the ancient forest, our enigmatic leader gives us simple instructions.

"Just keep taking the track to the left, never to the right. You can walk for two hours or twenty minutes, you choose. I'll be waiting for you here."

I've brought a backpack with every possible thing I might need from extra layers to extra water: food for about two days, a book and a torch. I'm laden. Nobody else seems to want to take anything on the hike. I look at Marcus as if to ask "What will I really need?" and he misunderstands my look.

"OK, OK," he says. "I'll come with you."

And off we set, Marcus hoisting my backpack onto his broad shoulders, me feeling a little sheepish. I'm not going to tell them I climbed three mountains in one week in Alaska not that long ago. The rain gets heavier. The trails are well made but exceptionally steep in places. The rainforest is a wonderland of shapes, colours, insects, wild flowers, berries, birds, streams and cascading waterfalls. It's incredible. Then we come to the three thousand year old alerce tree. I think we're all overwhelmed. It's an extraordinary feeling, touching something that existed before the Bible or the Koran or Buddhist scriptures.

We then get muddier and muddier. I'm drenched but have found an ally. Marcus thinks his mission for today is to take care of me. By the time we get to Santa Barbara beach we're all filthy, soaked to the skin and a team. The dolphins greet us. About thirty are playing in groups of four or five. The water is calm, dark blue-grey. These wonderful creatures are just thirty feet away from us. The sun sets. Trees become silhouettes. A new moon slides into view. A middle-aged farmer wearing thick sheepskin trousers rides bareback across the top of the beach. His horse is skittish. I look for the purple shells with the silver tips. Sylvie comes and sits on a rock beside me and in this small but intimate gesture of sharing, I feel such a fondness for her I allow myself a moment of sadness to think how life could have been had my daughter lived to be her age.

THE NEXT MORNING Raf, Sylvie and I are sitting in the minibus waiting for it to leave for Puyuhuapi. Out of Andres's office darts a beautiful slightly dark-skinned four year old chasing a puppy who wants to get into our bus.

"No, no, no," she yells in Spanish then in English. "Stay here with me!" Her sister is shyer but equally enchanting.

"They've both got Andres's eyes," says Sylvie, "don't you think? Look, so brown, and the little one's his spitting image. Don't you think so, Meg? You awake?"

I feel my disappointment turn to stone as I realise these are Andres's children and I seem to be the only person who hasn't noticed he's married. The legend bounds out of his wooden hut and asks us how the trip was yesterday. He's asking everybody but staring at me.

"Ciamar a tha thu?" he says to me with a lovely smile.

"Tha gu math!" I say back as brightly as I can. I had taught him "How are you?" and "I'm fine!" in Scottish Gaelic before we last parted.

"You'll love Puyuhuapi," he enthuses.

His eyes keep coming back to mine and staying there. I feel an emptiness in my heart which has nothing to do with him, but everything to do with my inability to attract available people.

AT THE TINY VILLAGE of Villa Santa Lucia, forty six kilometres south of Chaiten, where the road forks left to Futaleufú, right to the south, we stop at the same muddy crossroads café where the best breakfast in Chile is served. I can hardly contain my excitement at the thought of eating these delicious little breakfast treats. But sadly the chubby owner with the cheerful apron has turned stony-faced and hasn't made any this morning. There's dryish bread and instant coffee at five times the price!

Chapter 10

THE MINIBUS DROPS US beside a tumbledown hostal in the middle of Puyuhuapi. After a brief loo stop, the bus continues to Coyhaique, the gateway to all southern destinations.

The word *fjord* stirs my imagination. I think of Norway and New Zealand, slithers of dark blue water with high mountains rising up on either side. But Puyuhuapi isn't like that at all. The village is built around the end of what seems to be a lake; it's very hard to believe this is actually the sea. The houses are small, all made of wood, and some look Austrian or German. Brightly-painted old boats lie moored by the sandy beach. All around the bay rise, not mountains, but forested hills. I decide to stay here two days, mainly because I'm fascinated to interview fifty eight year old Lena, daughter of one of the four original pioneers who created the village.

Lena lives in Casa Hopman, her family home, now a guest house, and that's where Raphael, Sylvie and I head. It's easy to find. Standing apart from the rest of the village, this huge wooden house, painted red, has obviously been designed by a German. We climb up a broad, steep, internal stair and are met by Jo, a tall, thin American with a long, grey ponytail. When he tells us the price is thirty pesos per night, Raphael and Sylvie wilt. Not in their budget, nor mine, except for emergencies or special occasions. I'm tired and am wishing for the umpteenth time I'd brought a backpack not a wheelie. I stay, they go. Jo shows me to my room and lights the fire in the huge living room. His shoulder-length hair suggests an alternative soul. He tells me he's a boat-builder, and is married to Lena, who is not here. She's in Puerto Montt for a few days.

The wood-panelled living room-cum-dining room with windows looking onto the fjord was the original village meeting place for many years. I pick up a magazine, and absorb some local information.

"The beautiful Carretera Austral [the road down which we have just driven from Chaiten] *was begun in 1976 with the aim of connecting Chile's extremities. The central section of Pinochet's grand Southern Highway opened in 1983, linking Coyhaique with Chaiten. Five years later it reached Puerto Montt in the north and Cochrane in the south. Stretching around a thousand kilometres, work on the road still continues. Torn between the need for progress and the desire for preservation, local people still debate whether the road is a good thing or not, but the fact is, it is here."*

Another article catches my attention.

"Notes on Patagonia. **Puyuhuapi**: *This is when I conquer my childhood fear of slime. The tree trunk that Patricio, my guide, is pointing to glistens with fungus, freak-coloured moss and god knows what else—but this is my hand-hold. Waterproofed from head to toe, we crossed a stormy fjord in a tiny rowing boat and have been clambering though lush rainforest that seethes with wild life, wading up streams and over moss-carpeted and lichen-covered logs, tight roping over makeshift bridges. I feel like one of the Famous Five. We emerge at a thundering waterfall and sit on a rock in the spray, soaking in the view of the dense green slopes and snow-dusted granite peaks. This place is worth getting up* *early for. For this abundance of wildness, Aisen* [the name of the province I'm now in] *has its total geographical isolation to thank and blame."*

WITHOUT BEING ASKED, Jo gives me info about the local luxury spa, how to get there, how to get to the hot springs and the glacier—they're all nearby. A man called Juan who owns the tumbledown hostal beside the bus shack will take visitors anywhere, for a fee. When I tell the quiet American about Casa Redonda, Andres comes into the conversation. He and Jo are old friends.

Is Andres the main character I'm looking for?

Why am I so *magnetically* drawn to him?

What makes him still so intriguing, so endearing, so elusive?

In mythology, heroes' wounds may not necessarily be visible. People put a great deal of energy into protecting and hiding their weak and vulnerable spots. Why will Andres never answer a straight question? Who can I pair him with? Because for certain sure it's not going be me. That's impossible. The angel in the tunnel—could he be her father? Marta? What connection could he have with her?

Jo drops a few nuggets of information about Andres into our conversation and I get a fascinating new picture of this mysterious character who loves to fish and who shares his problems with another North American immigrant. Having kids has changed him, Jo concludes. In what way, I ask? No comment! Jo has disappeared.

Will I delete Andres from the possible cast list now?

It seems I can't.

The next morning I meet Raf and Sylvie who've had a rough night. They found a cheap hostal where they could

cook, but the owners weren't friendly. They're waiting for
the bus south to Cochrane. I feel an inexplicable sadness in
saying goodbye to these two young lovers.

"Suerte," says Raf, good luck.

Sylvie hugs me.

MY NEW HOME for the next few nights will be an
enchanting little wooden hut that looks like the three bears
have just vacated it. There's a steep ladder connecting the
tiny sitting room to the loft, where three beds with pretty
quilts and little bedside tables sit side by side. The bedroom
window looks down onto a small, overgrown garden full
of tall swaying wild pink flowers. Behind the pink lies the
ultramarine fjord; behind the fjord lies the south of Patagonia
and Tortel, which is now eight days away. I will arrive there
possibly around the twenty sixth of March, two days away
from the date the astrologer has warned me about.

Vera's award-winning café is built beside the teddy bears'
cabins. It's a successful business, by the look if it. There's
a photo of her on the wall, smiling beside a middle-aged
government official. She offers simple meals and rents the
chalets for reasonable prices during the summer. In winter,
like Lorinda, she goes back to Santiago and shuts up shop.
Vera is shy, capable and slightly secretive.

I'm looking for Juan to see if I can visit the nearby hot
springs. He's easy to find, everybody knows him. We
arrange to meet at three o'clock and I have an extremely
bizarre lunch, thanks to some second guessing.

The restaurant in the main street facing the fjord is also a
shop and a hostal. To get to the restaurant you have to walk
though a door at the back of the shop. Even at this time of
day the shop is dark. It sells everything the villagers might

need: fruit, frozen meat, bread, tea, coffee, beer, waterproofs, batteries, eggs, toys, light bulbs. At about ten thirty, I ask for a coffee and am offered a seat in the dining room downstairs; I presume the hostal is upstairs. I have my coffee and say I'd like to come back for lunch.

"Fine," says the owner.

Naturally I sit myself down at the same table for lunch, and the family begins to return, one by one. Vegetable soup is put in front of me. The father of the house arrives and looks intently at my bowl. Second course arrives, fish and boiled potatoes, grandmother arrives. She studies my plate. Everybody watches me like I'm eating poisoned produce or frogs legs. They all keep looking at my face then at my plate.

"Dessert?" asks the cook.

"No, thank you," I say. As I leave the table, which is set for many people, the family swoop around it. With a flash of embarrassment I realise the restaurant must be upstairs. I've kept the family waiting for their meal for approximately twenty minutes. I wish they could have just joined me.

JUAN DRIVES SKILFULLY in and around the potholes as we make our way to the alternative hot springs. When we arrive, the gate's bolted and there's nobody there.

"I think the owner's gone away!" he says.

Did he know this before we set off? He's grinning a lot.

As we drive back to Puyuhuapi, I ask if it would be possible to visit the famous luxury spa. How much would it cost to get there, could I go this afternoon?

Juan says he could call them. The last boat leaves the spa at six, so there isn't much time. Back at his office, a phone call alerts the health resort that a guest will be arriving soon and the boat is sent to pick me up.

We set off again in Juan's old four-by-four, up the same potholed road past the closed hot springs and, seventeen kilometres later, we wait at the jetty for the small power boat to pick me up. It's a speck in the distance. A radio phone call to the skipper ascertains he's on his way, but he's just been down the fjord to Puyuhuapi to collect me there while we've been driving up here. Juan's having a good day out of this innocent visitor!

It's a five minute speed trip across the fjord in a small motorboat to get to the spa. I'm greeted by young and cheerful Marisol, who explains how the place works. It's now five and the last boat leaves the spa at six. I have exactly one hour for this next adventure. While waiting at the jetty I've studied the list of massages and beauty treatments on offer. I ask about the chocolate and orange head massage.

"Sorry, not available," I'm told with a cheeky grin.

Marisol persuasively offers me something else involving chocolate and orange, but I don't quite get it.

"Ok," I say. "That's fine!"

I have no idea what I'm letting myself in for. Although this is called a luxury resort, it's not intimidating. It's posh but friendly and Marisol's funny.

Five minutes after arriving, I'm flopping about like a happy turtle in a hot spring pool in water that's about thirty eight degrees. From the pool, the landscape all around is stunning. I can see, almost touch, the fjord; it's just feet away. I see the Cyprus forests rising on the shore opposite. The sky is cloudless. I hear the water lapping gently against the rocks. Squirrels dart between trees. Leaves rustle, the water is bliss. It's all bliss. There's nobody else around, although there's a group of four Israeli students in one of the other pools further down the wooded track.

Twenty minutes later Marisol appears as arranged. She takes me to the main part of the spa which looks like a James Bond movie set, circa 1970. I'm handed over to Myte for the chocolate and orange experience. She leads me along a narrow, prison-like, iron walkway overlooking two empty, indoor aquamarine pools. There's a wall of thirty foot high glass between us and the fjord. Cyprus trees grow all around the wooden complex.

We arrive at a small cream-coloured room, cell-like, with a high window. Myte lights a candle. She flicks an Enya tape into action, which disorientates me immediately. I stare with terror at the huge machine that takes up most of the room. It's like a gigantic thermos flask that's opened down the middle. Inside is a mattress covered with a white sheet. Where's the massage table I'm wondering? Enya drones, the candle fills the air with a beautiful fragrance. I look at Myte and try to decide if I've made a terrible mistake.

"Take off all your clothes and lie on the mattress," she says smiling. I'm not smiling at this point.

Twenty minutes later I've survived the vigorous rubbing in of pounded chocolate and gritty ground, dried orange skins all over my body. I've also survived the encasing in the thermos flask, head sticking out at the top for ten minutes to sweat; then more rubbing and pummelling. I leave to catch the little blue speed boat across the narrow fjord where Juan is waiting for me. I'm glowing and scented with orange. I flop into the boat with a delicious feeling of having been deeply cleansed, my body softened like piece of dough in the hands of a skilled master.

VERA'S SUPPER of pasta with pesto sauce is tasty but it's her dessert that's unforgettable. Chocolate terrine with cranberries and cream. Her little café-restaurant is empty except for me, so we chat and she tells me she'll soon be locking up and returning to Santiago for the winter. There's a story here I'm sure, but it's too soon for it to emerge. Her handsome, teenage kitchen-hand, Juanito, dries dishes in a dark corner of the back room, beside the sink. He watches Vera intently.

I leave her, still smelling of chocolate and orange, to sleep sweetly in the three bears' cabin.

Chapter 11

THE BUS TO COYHAIQUE (the next stretch of the Carretera Austral) will leave at one o'clock in the afternoon, so there's time to explore more of Puyuhuapi. Wandering around the village I notice surely the smallest restaurant in the world, right beside the shore. It's a black wooden shack, like an allotment shed, surrounded by an abundant luscious vegetable garden. On a piece of wood nailed above the door, the word *cocinera*—cook—is written in child-like script. I make a mental note that if ever possible, I will return to have a meal there.

Further around the shoreline, a track winds towards the rug factory.

This famous little wooden establishment was built in 1940 by the group of four intrepid German pioneers who first sailed into the fjord in 1935. One of them, Walter Hopperdietzel, had a textile factory back in Germany. Their objective was to start producing carpets as soon as possible, and this they did. They cleared the land, built their homes, brought workers down from the island of Chiloé, trained them, but first they shipped in skilled craftsmen from Germany to build the looms. Local sheep provided an abundance of the raw material. It was a success story. Rugs were sold to shops in Santiago and Germany. Today rugs and carpets are still made here and shipped all over the world.

A string of old, Austrian-looking, weathered wooden houses line the road. What a pity Lena, who grew up in the village as it evolved, isn't here today. She will remember so much of how things used to be. And what was her mother's story? How did she meet the intrepid pioneer Herr Hopman? How did he die aged just fifty eight? Could my story be in here somewhere?

Inside the 'factory', shafts of sunlight illuminate a huge, wooden shed. There are two floors connected by a dark staircase. Downstairs, the enormous looms lie quiet and empty, except for one which is manned by a native woman, bored by being peered at and endlessly photographed. Upstairs in a large showroom, a heavy folder shows a collection of photos and samples of the rugs which have been sent around the world to wealthy customers. The designs are impressive. You can even design your own carpet nowadays, and they'll make it for a price. Across the road is another wooden building where most of the rugs are being made. I'm told eleven people work there, but I don't have time to visit. The bus is due.

I reckon I'm only two, possibly three, nights away from Tortel now. My sense of mission is escalating.

THE BUS ARRIVES. It's a twelve-seater; a dusty, well-used institution. All the way to Coyhaique, the policeman we picked up outside Puyuhuapi police station talks to our bus driver. They sit side by side. The policeman's wiry, about thirty four, thin, dark-haired. Usually there's a sign which says it's illegal to talk to the driver while he's driving, but our bus doesn't have this. The police station was all of fifty yards from the bus depot, but our man didn't want to join our queue. He wanted special treatment right from the start. The dynamic between our driver and the plain-clothes policeman is firstly irritating, then distressing, then infuriating. As we drive though magnificent scenery with the Andes rising to incredible heights on our left, passing rivers gushing though wild unfenced land, massive plants—cousins of the rhubarb family—lining either side of the dirt track road, the policeman talks non-stop. I'm sitting right behind him. He seems incapable of pausing, let alone stopping. Our polite and self-effacing driver, or possibly our nervous driver, is sucked into a drama from which there is no escape. Many sick bags are filled and chucked out of the windows.

MY GUIDEBOOK TELLS ME: *"Coyhaique lies in a broad green valley four hundred and twenty kilometres south of Chaiten. The city is encircled by a crown of snow-capped mountains and, for a few hours after it's rained, the mountainsides are covered in a fine layer of frost, a spectacular sight."*

What I see through the dusty bus window as daylight disappears, is a town in the distance on a ridge. I can't see any frosted mountains and I've no sense of being encircled, but there's a huge sense of relief and excitement at reaching this destination. The thrill is short-lived.

Arriving in Coyhaique my nerves appear to be frazzled and it's almost dark. A bad combination. Everybody disappears from the bus yard quickly. Suddenly I feel overtaken by a profound exhaustion. For once I haven't booked a bed in advance, anywhere. The bus office is a shack on a bit of wasteland behind us. I'll ask for help. The receptionist is a tired young woman in a bad mood, wanting to lock up and go home. I check the guidebook and ask if she can call a taxi.

"There's no need," she informs me. "There are lots of hostals in O'Higgins Street."

She hands me a small brochure with tiny print. This isn't much help because I'm well past deciphering a map and remembering directions. I'm breaking one of my most important travel rules: never arrive in a city after dark without a booking.

The taxi arrives. We drive down a busy main street, then start zigzagging around blocks. Soon we arrive in a seedy, dimly-lit wide street and I'm shocked to see a grubby sign which says Hostal Neena beside what looks like a junkyard. This is my destination.

"This is it," smiles the driver, and plonks my wheelie on the pavement.

He disappears. I feel nervous, then daunted, then survival mode kicks in.

HOSTAL NEENA is at the bottom of an unlit track, off an uninviting road lined by discarded, ancient junk. It's rated in the guidebook as good value. There's a rundown hairdresser's salon and a dirty sign for a laundrette at the entrance to the lane. The track has no lighting at all. I pull my suitcase on wheels (who, at some point, I've decided to call Shamus) across uneven ruts and my heart sinks as I get closer to the building. A lace curtain moves. A voice shouts "¡Otra puerta!"—"Other door!" As instructed, I open a door and walk into an unlit small shed, filled with debris and sacks of something. A door off it opens.

Suddenly I find myself in a kitchen full of light. Neena sits at a long table peeling rosehips. There's a mountain of scarlet berries beside her and a large aluminium pot. She has long, wild hair which hides half her face, a shifty look, is about sixty and has a slightly witchy grin.

She shows me the only bedroom that's available. It has a window looking into the entrance shed I just came through. The bedroom is high, dimly lit, with two single beds. The wardrobe is covered with children's stickers, half peeled off and scratched, and the floor has brown linoleum. The bathroom is steamy with a green lino floor and an old shower. For a moment I assess the risk factors of staying here. *Could put the wardrobe in front of the door and escape through the window into the lane if necessary, I think.*

"OK," I say. "Thank you."

It's too late to go anywhere else.

"Have a cup of tea then," grins Neena.

We sit in her kitchen drinking strong tea. The TV blares. We eye each other.

She tells me making rosehip jam is Chinese labour. She asks me where I just came from.

"Puyuhuapi," I say.

"Where did you stay?" she asks.

"At Casa Hopman. I wanted to 'interview' Lena, the daughter of one of those four famous pioneers, but she wasn't there, my bad luck she was in Puerto Montt."

"That's right," says Neena. "She was, but she's here now. You'll meet her at breakfast."

From Neena, I discover all the things I need for my journey to Tortel are close by: a supermarket, a bank, a launderette. She gives me minimal information about the buses. What needs to be done tomorrow is to navigate the confusion of the various small bus companies which head south for Tortel. Some go on Monday, Wednesday and Saturday; others Wednesday and Sunday.

THE NIGHT PASSES with not too much sleep and at breakfast Lena appears. She's about fifty eight, small, slim and not interested in yet another set of questions about her extraordinary father. She's polite, but not interested in making conversation, so I'm left wondering why she would want to stay in Neena's hostal for six pesos a night when she charges thirty at her B&B. Maybe Neena's a *Very Interesting Person?* Maybe scary Neena is the guardian of my story? Her large husband likes to lie stretched out like a well-fed cat on the bench behind the woodstoves and doze. The bench, with its long cushion, looks like it's been specially built for this purpose. Lying there he gets the heat and he also gets to see who's coming down the garden path. His is the hand that twitches the lace curtain.

GANGS OF WILD DOGS patrol the main street of Coyhaique. They're not so much menacing as amusing. Roaming around in motley groups, they scavenge rubbish bins and trot down the main street carrying bulging plastic bags in their mouths. The grassy, pentagonal plaza nearby seems to be their favourite place to feast.

In the early afternoon I'm trying to find the bus depot for southern departures. There are four bus companies in town. It's extremely confusing getting any kind of information as to where they are. Turning up tomorrow without a ticket is not advised by Neena. It could lead to a two-day wait. My next stop is going to be Rio Tranquilo, a small village on the shores of Chile's second largest lake.

I finally find the correct bus depot and buy my travel document; once again I have to supply my passport number. I've heard there are some wonderful marble caves at Rio Tranquilo and an overnight stay there will break the long journey to Cochrane. I'm two nights away from Tortel now, I think.

Around the main plaza in Coyhaique there's a kind of mini village of wooden huts for craftspeople to display their wares. Some huts have a small workshop; others are just full of carvings, knitwear, ceramics or jewellery. In one, a window displaying stones of all sizes with beautiful animals and indigenous symbols engraved in white, lines catches my eye. A few paintings line the inside walls. Huge crystals and beautiful gemstones lie everywhere on dusty surfaces. I notice a small bench in the semi-darkness, heaped with the craftsman's tools. There's a packet of cigarettes and a jersey on top of a well-used canvas stool. The craftsman/woman's a smoker and autumn is on its way here. This hut is an Aladdin's cave of creativity.

Drawing on stones. I feel myself getting extremely excited about this art form. Javier the craftsman appears. He's about fifty five, weathered, tired and exceptionally talented. We chat and exchange websites. I'd really love to buy something, but he's giving me high-season, tourist prices. I tell him I'm hoping to come back next year. This doesn't change anything. And why should it?

I'm not captivated by Coyhaique and the prospect of another night at Neena's isn't great. There are no banking facilities further south now for Visa cards, so if you run out of money from this point on, you're in serious trouble. In Tortel a plane flies in once a month with banking services, but Visa cards aren't catered for. A trip to the local supermarket provides food for the journey and I withdraw enough money for the next two weeks. A collection of little worry-thoughts starts lining up in my head. What if I get stranded? I won't. Sure? Yes! What if—? No *what ifs* on this trip please, just Plan B. What if I lose all my money? Get robbed! You won't. Have you ever? What about the *crisis*? And the looming twenty eighth of March? What's going to happen? Shhhhhh!

I get my clothes washed at the launderette and am amused to see my jeans, socks and orange jacket hanging on somebody's clothesline in the garden beside Neena's house. I'm set for Tortel now and at eight thirty the next morning, I'm waiting to board the bus to Rio Tranquilo.

Chapter 12

IN THE SMALL, BUT BUSY, BUS DEPOT I notice a young couple carrying a vast array of bags all shapes and sizes. They're not dressed in the usual uniform of youthful world travellers: hiking boots, fleeces, Gore-Tex jackets. He wears a brown, hand-knitted Peruvian hat with pigtails, striped trousers, trainers and a heavy jacket. She wears black from top to toe and sunglasses. They board our bus.

Our seats are numbered. Beside me, in almost the front row, sits a beautiful twelve year old girl. Her mother is busy organising everything they will need for the 462 kilometre journey to Cochrane. The child's wheelchair has been folded and stuffed in the back with the other luggage. Her fourteen year old brother sits in front of her. She asks me my name and I say "Margarita". Chileans and Spaniards can't say "Meg", they say something like "Ek" or "Egg", whilst they say "Margarita" beautifully.

"Mar-gar-it-a," she says slowly, with a heart-melting smile.

"And yours?" I ask.

"Nadine," she says, and her head flops onto her chest.

Nadine is paralysed from the chest down. She and her mum have obviously made this journey many times before, probably for hospital visits. The bus begins to fill up. Nadine's mum is preparing for all possibilities: their food bag on the floor, sick bags on top of the food bag, water bottle, towel, windows opened, roof window opened. Nadine's mum pops a sweetie in her daughter's mouth, then one in her own. The child smiles at her mother, then at me. The driver climbs aboard and hands out blue plastic sick bags to anyone who wants one. Most people accept.

As we speed down the next stretch of the Carretera Austral towards Rio Tranquilo and Cochrane, the road becomes extremely twisty and steep. The sick bags begin to fill up. Nadine's mother tucks a towel under her daughter's chin and over her shoulders. When finally poor Nadine does throw up, her mother has the plastic bag perfectly positioned and once full, she opens the window wider, chucks out the bag, heaves her daughter onto the seat beside the window, sticks her head half out of the window, readjusts the towel, pops a sweetie in her own mouth and settles down for a few minutes till the next manoeuvre is required. Moments later, Nadine needs water and her mouth wiped. Mum rearranges Nadine's legs and puts them in the lotus position. Nadine has stopped smiling but still looks beautiful. Almost everybody in the bus is throwing up. It's a complete miracle I'm not part of this collective travel sickness.

AFTER A FEW HOURS, we stop at a small village in front of the magnificent Cerro Castillo Mountain. We're in another National Reserve named after its mountain, which looks like a fairytale castle jutting out from a covering of snow. Nearby are caves whose rock paintings are estimated to be around ten thousand years old.

The bus pulls to a halt, sick bags are disposed of. We all pile out for a loo and food stop. Not much food gets eaten. Nadine is lifted out and seated on the grassy verge beside the road. Her brother becomes her attentive carer while her mother and I head for the toilets.

A pretty young woman wearing traveller's gear, clutching the fat *Lonely Planet South America on a Shoestring*, waits as we all pile off the bus. She tries to board.

"No, no," says our driver. "Wait."

When we leave fifteen minutes later, our new passenger mimes to the driver to stop at the top of the road to pick up her mother.

The scenery continues to be sublime. Nadine and most of the other passengers continue to throw up. Nadine's mum continues to look after her daughter, never resting for more than a few moments all the way to Puerto Tranquilo, our next stop. This is where the bus refuels and everybody has lunch, either in the little café beside the gas station, or beside the lake with a picnic.

As we approach the village, we skirt Largo General Carrera, one of Chile's most famous lakes. This section of the Carretera Austral around the north and western sides of the lake is reckoned to be the most spectacular stretch of the entire thousand kilometre journey. Straddling the frontier with Argentina, the lake is the largest in South America after Lake Titicaca, and is believed to be the deepest on the continent. The region is said to have three hundred days of sunshine every year. Today it's blustery.

Sixteen of us pile out of the bus. The young couple with the mass of luggage, the mother and daughter (still clutching the *Lonely Planet* guide) and I ask for our bags. The five of us, it seems, are going to stop here overnight.

Across this incredibly deep lake lies Argentina, with all her beauty and all her tragic turbulent past, faint in the far distance like an apparition. The water is the colour of pure turquoise. It's actually turquoise as far as the eye can see. Nearby lie the famous marble caves. They've been gouged slowly, little by little, out of a narrow peninsula, by wild waters over centuries of seasons.

THE MOTHER AND DAUGHTER TEAM, Ashley and Lindsey, who are from New Zealand, have already consulted their *Lonely Planet* bible and set off briskly to find a hostal they say sounds good and cheap.

The young couple, Rachel and Jerome, with their twenty bags, are French. Rachel and I hover beside the bus together, exchanging bits of information and smiles. We choose to speak in Spanish. She's an artist from an aristocratic background and he's a musician and teacher of circus skills to street children. Something's going to happen here. I feel it coming. There's a story about to unfold. The couple have just left Bolivia in a hurry. Something went seriously wrong there. I think a child has died.

"Are you here to visit the marble caves?" I ask when Jerome joins us.

"Yes, briefly," he replies.

"What's Bolivia like?" I wish I could elaborate on my question, but I can't, I'm slightly nervous of Jerome and I don't yet know why.

"Bolivia?" he asks as if he's never been there.

"Yes, is it—is it like Chile?"

"No."

"Is it—are there more indigenous people there—? How long did you live there?"

"Too long."

"Oh!"

Jerome doesn't move away. I think it's not that he doesn't want to talk; it's more that he doesn't want to remember.

"Bolivia's a difficult place to live," chips in Rachel. "There's so much violence between the different people."

"Violence?"

"Yes—and poverty and street kids and corruption. Lots of huge social problems."

"We were teaching," Jerome suddenly decides to talk to me.

"We did the very best we could, but it wasn't enough. It was terrible what was happening. The political situation is— is killing men, women and children every day, every day."

I look at their pile of bags. Yes, they are relocating.

"I arrived two years ago," Rachel tells me. "Jerome has lived in Bolivia for four years." She hides her expression behind dark glasses.

"They have women wrestlers in Bolivia," Rachel continues. "Did you know that? It's amazing. One woman represents all the vile forces in the world and the other tries to hammer her, not to death, but into submission, like a serious, terrible punishing."

I remember my chocolate factory days.

"The crowd absolutely love seeing evil punished. The women wrestlers are very popular. Sometimes the fights start up again outside the ring. I was always so frightened for the children of the wrestlers, that their moms would be killed. And the street demonstrations. Very, very dangerous places."

"Did you see these wrestling matches?"

"Yes, a few times. I couldn't bear it actually. Maybe it's like bull fighting in Spain. You have to grow up with the concept in your psyche."

"We've left behind a lot," Jerome tells me.

"We're going to start all over again—in Argentina, probably."

I discover Rachel and Jerome are also heading for Tortel. Leaving their mountain of bags by the roadside, they say "¡Hasta luego!"—"See you later!"—and wander off towards the lake. I ask at the small petrol station where to find a bed for the night.

After checking out a few possibilities and finding them to be in the Hostal Neena category, I decide to pay double and have a comfortable night with a room overlooking the turquoise lake. Feeling hungry, I wander back towards the café and meet Ashley and Lindsey who've just had a bowl of soup there. They tell me their hostal is OK.

"It's a bit—how shall we say?—basic, but it's cheap."

They're exploring five South American countries on a tight budget and a tight timetable; they're here to visit the marble caves. We swap information about the boat to the caves and agree to rendezvous later to arrange our adventure. The boatman's called Lenin, they say, he's a bit of a colourful character. His office is the old caravan opposite the petrol pump. He rents cabins on the beach too, wildly expensive apparently.

"Maybe the French couple would like to come to the caves, too," Ashley suggests.

"The more the cheaper probably," adds her mother.

Mother and daughter disappear to explore the nearby waterfalls.

APPROACHING the petrol station again, which has just one stocky, old-fashioned pump and a small painted shed beside it, I see Rachel and Jerome. They're sitting on the white sand beside the turquoise lake, shoulders propped against each other, about a hundred yards from where I stop. They've eaten lunch. The remnants of their picnic—bread, fruit and a bottle of water—lie on Jerome's jacket. It's a squally day.

Whilst I take this information in, silently and gracefully Rachel gets up, unhurriedly. She glides to the left in a kind of slow motion dance, arms outstretched, toes pointed, her slim body a black silhouette against the turquoise water. Jerome watches her. Time stands still. Birds circle overhead. A wild horse grazes nearby. Jerome rises effortlessly, clown-like, dreamily and in slow motion stretches and begins an exquisite series of movements on the fine, white sand. It's not tai chi and it's not karate. It's something in-between. I think he's making it up. Rachel's dance becomes more exotic, more dream-like, more surreal, faster, slower, she doesn't stop. Now she's cart-wheeling, spinning into the turquoise water. The water responds to her movements. White froth rings her ankles and wrists. Billowing clouds chase each other northwards. Just around the corner, just out of sight, wait the alluring marble caves. And on the other side of the lake, Argentina watches like a stoic, silent, far-away witness.

It's as if these two lovers are telling the world a story; their story. Without words, without music, a tragic fairy tale unfolds, a modern myth comes to life, a contemporary legend explains itself. My creative imagination is torched. The essence of my film has arrived.

I don't want it to stop. I stand captivated, witnessing pure theatre and a feeling of excitement I'd forgotten was possible. I'm spinning inside with all of these feelings and thoughts and images while Jerome continues to lance an army of a thousand invisible warriors and Rachel continues to cartwheel into the turquoise waves.

I've found my main characters! I've found them. I can build on this—and yes!—I know there's so much more to come. I knew I'd find my story in Patagonia. Here is where it all starts.

Inside, my creative spirit is shooting with the stars.

Chapter 13

A FEW HOURS LATER I meet my four new travelling companions in the wooden café beside the one-pump petrol station. I'm quietly ecstatic. I can't stop smiling. We drink tea and swap notes about the marble caves and our plans. Ashley, a peripatetic physiotherapist, is about twenty six; bright, bubbly and full of energy. She's a planner and a strategist. Lindsey, her mother, is quiet, observant and a primary school teacher. Lindsey explains that her husband hates to travel, so she gets to explore all sorts of exotic places with her daughter. Last year they travelled around southern China together. They've already found our boatman Lenin and agreed a fair price. We'll leave tomorrow morning at nine they say. It's only twenty minutes by boat down the lake to the caves. Our bus leaves for Cochrane at midday.

Jerome and Rachel have opted for the grimmest hostal in the village. Ashley, Lindsey and I had already checked it out. My rating was five notches worse than Neena's.

"We can cook there," says Jerome seriously. "This is important for us."

"Do you enjoy cooking?" Lindsay inquires innocently.

Jerome appears not to hear the question.

"We're living on fruit and sandwiches mainly," Ashley volunteers.

"Where have you just come from?" asks Lindsey.

"Bolivia," replies Rachel.

"Ah, Bolivia," sighs Ashley. "Fascinating country, we didn't have long there but we saw the salt plains."

Silence.

"We were teaching in Bolivia," Jerome surprises me by sharing this info with Lindsey and Ashley. I'd sensed he decided to keep quiet. Maybe the drama on the beach had cleared something for him.

"We need to find a new country, different kind of work and a new place to live now."

His English is faltering. I can't see Rachel's eyes. Her sunglasses seem glued to her face. We discover we're all heading for Tortel with the same sense of intense mission and adventure.

AT NINE THE NEXT MORNING, we meet our boatman Lenin in front of his ancient, cream-coloured caravan which sits opposite the petrol station/café/bus halt. The caravan's a kind of landmark. Lenin grins into the far distance but doesn't say much. We follow him out of the village, past a group of beautiful wooden cabins on the beach—which he owns and rents out—to the jetty where his boat is moored. It's a kind of a rowing boat with an outboard motor. The day is bright but breezy.

Our first sighting of the marble caves makes me think that a surrealist sculptor and an abstract painter have been working here together.

Ashley sits in the bow, camera poised. Lenin switches off the engine and our little boat glides into a turquoise cave. The roof is just a few feet above our heads. There are only inches spare on either side of the boat. The peninsula is a mass of narrow, low, deep caves, each one with beautiful rock formations sculpted by nature over countless centuries.

Each cave is a combination of different shades of turquoise blue, dull purples and browns.

We glide in and out. I wonder who first found the caves. Then, without warning, Lenin yanks the boat around and we race across another stretch of turquoise water towards more caves. Another peninsula. Here we go in deeper. Now we see a cave which leaves us speechless. It's beyond description. Superlatives don't work. This is nature at her most extraordinary. Then, unexpectedly, while we are still soaking in the unforgettable beauty of the cave, hypnotised with awe, Lenin switches on the engine, swivels the boat around roughly and we charge off wildly into an upcoming storm. Where did all this wind come from?

Lenin becomes a daredevil. The wind tosses our little boat right up on its end then it crashes down in between waves only to be thrown up again and tossed back down. Our 'captain' keeps near to the shore and I'm glad of this because I'm fairly sure we're going to be in the water soon, and the water could be 590 metres deep. I reckon I could just swim to the rocks from here, but only if I can remove my hiking boots first. No chance with the boots on. I spend the next ten minutes wondering about untying my boots in preparation. Will I—won't I? We get soaked with spray and somehow drowning in turquoise feels like an OK way to go.

By the time we land we've become an elastic little group. The sun shines as we roam back silently to our different hostals. There are a few hours to fill before the bus arrives.

An hour later, a breathless Ashley knocks on my door saying: "The bus has arrived early, hurry they won't wait, tell Jerome and Rachel!"

I run to the grim hostal but Rachel and Jerome aren't there. At the bus stop I find Ashley looking sheepish.

"Sorry," she says. "My Spanish is awful. It was the bus going in the opposite direction that arrived. It's just left."

"Never mind," I say. "Doesn't matter."

It turns out to be Lindsey's birthday, so I treat them to a coffee in the roadside café.

Our next stop on the way to Tortel is Cochrane. We're getting very close. Just one more night and we'll be there. We swap info about Tortel over coffee.

BACK ON THE MINIBUS, blue plastic sick bags are handed out again. The road twists and winds through more unforgettable scenery. The wide, sand-coloured dirt track road is lined with a seemingly never-ending forest of gigantic wild green rhubarb plants. They are least five feet tall, maybe more. At the back of them, a higher level of trees makes a dense impenetrable wall for humans. This is real wilderness territory, just feet away from the road. Behind the trees, the Andes rise magnificently. Here and there, five hundred foot waterfalls spill down mountainsides like cans of white paint tipped and allowed to dribble slowly. The sky is cloudless. Rivers are opal-coloured. Wild horses graze peacefully. Condors fly overhead. The occasional remote homestead we pass makes me want to get off the bus and meet the kind of people who can endure this kind of isolation. Each homestead looks like a film set waiting to be shot. But who are the characters? What secrets do they hide? What joys, tragedies, what dramas have unfolded here? A man on horseback waves as we pass. How can I get close to these stories?

LAKE GENERAL CARERRA

Meg Robinson

MARBLE CAVES AT RIO TRANQUILO

Chapter 14

WHEN WE ARRIVE AT COCHRANE it's fascinating to observe how our little group goes about finding a bed for the night. Once again, Ashley and Lindsey have consulted the *Lonely Planet* bible. They head off briskly for their pre-chosen budget accommodation. Rachel and Jerome deposit their many bags in a little mountain on the pavement and look around. One of them will stay guard while the other searches for a room with cooking facilities.

I ask the young woman at the bus shack for a recommendation. Our driver says he always stays at Hostal San Marco.

"Very good and very near," he assures me, looking at my wheelie. The friendly Girl Friday makes a phone call.

"Yes," she says, "they have a room." She gives me directions. I come close to Hostal San Marco and that familiar NO makes itself heard loudly. It's a new white modern concrete building with a huge satellite dish.

Seeing a small sign at the end of a road stretching out in front of me, I carry on walking. It's the far end edge of the village. Chickens scramble around in the middle of the dirt road. An elderly smartly dressed lady walks slowly towards me studying me carefully.

"Are you looking for my hostal?" she asks in Spanish.

TEN MINUTES LATER I'M FIXED UP IN RESIDENCIAL JUANJO. Seventy year old Carla has tried to sell me her posh expensive room with en-suite bathroom, but I'm happier with the rustic option which has a lovely view of the garden and purple mountains behind. Carla brings me a plate of red apples from her garden. I'm so grateful because it's hours since I ate. Her garden is full of pink roses and yellow honeysuckle. After a welcome shower in a Hostal Neena-style bathroom, Carla offers me tea in her sitting room.

This elderly, well-dressed, European-looking widow is a natural storyteller. Her family arrived from Germany two generations ago.

"I'm Chilean," she says proudly, "not German."

Her beloved husband Juanjo died ten years ago.

"Of a heart attack," she says. "Very quick. Best way to go."

Finally she's found peace and contentment running her little guest house, looking after her garden, making jam and sewing. She's a natural storyteller.

She tells me aged twenty one, searching for a place to call home, she and her young German pioneer husband went into a drinking den in the middle of nowhere. Hungry, tired and thirsty after many days riding with their horse and cart, the half-dozen wild men at the makeshift bar just *stared* at her, speechless and menacing.

"Fifty years ago," she says, "I was a beautiful, young, city woman from Buenos Aires looking for adventure. I might as well have arrived from another planet. They just stared and stared at me. Nobody said anything. My husband asked for a drink for us. Finally, a filthy hand belonging to an unwashed person passed me a mug of *mate*. Their stares turned into grins. Would I or wouldn't I drink it? I was horrified. You know what *mate* is, Margarita?"

"Sort of," I say.

"*Mate*," explains Carla, "is the Argentinean national drink."

Wherever you go in Argentina, you'll see groups of people sharing a *mate* (pronounced mattay). Whatever their class, everyone drinks several *mates* a day. It's dried yerba leaves, similar to tea. The leaves are placed in a hollowed-out gourd, into which hot water is poured; the infusion is drunk through a metal straw with a filter at the bottom. The cup is topped up with hot water for each person in the group. Everybody drinks from the same straw. Carla says she nearly died at the thought of drinking from the same straw as those cowboys. But with true grit she drank the lot then asked for a whisky.

"To kill the germs," she tells me.

I need more information about the bus to Tortel tomorrow so I leave Carla with her freshly excavated memories.

"Come back any time," she smiles. "The key's under the flower pot."

IN COCHRANE'S ONLY SUPERMARKET, I search for something for supper that doesn't need cooking. This store has a feel of times gone by. Dried foods sit in large brown sacks. The floor is grey cement. There are metal units making three aisles in the centre of this barn-like building. Wheelbarrows, pails, saws, nails, string, paint, clothes, toys, food, electrical goods, iron stoves, shoes and more fill sagging shelves.

I bump into Ashley and Lindsey buying fruit for tomorrow's journey, then Rachel and Jerome buying cheese and eggs. Ashley tells Rachel they're looking for a restaurant noted in *The Lonely Planet* to celebrate Lindsey's birthday, which was yesterday. Tonight they want a nice meal and pisco. *Pisco* is the national drink they inform me.

"Come and join us," they say. Rachel and Jerome decide they'll just come for a drink. They've already bought bread and cheese and fruit for supper. Rachel's still wearing her shades.

After a few wrong turns, we find the famous café-restaurant on the edge of town. Ashley orders two piscos and explains it's a spirit made from grapes, usually drunk with lemon or lime juice. I join them. After half a glass on an empty stomach I feel totally drunk. I hear myself telling all sorts of extraordinary stories including some of Carla's with a bit of dramatic embellishment. After the second pisco, while we still wait for our food, I give Lindsey the little birthday gift I found in the supermarket. It's a box of chocolates made in the shape of hammers! There wasn't much of a choice I tell her. She says she loves chocolates and quickly stuffs the box in her backpack. Oh dear, I think, I was hoping that might have been our tapas. The food finally arrives and it's delicious.

The next morning, my head feeling slightly fuzzy, we meet up again and join a small group of people waiting for the bus to Tortel. Ashley and Lindsey confess their hostal wasn't great.

"Very basic," they say.

Rachel and Jerome struck lucky and were able to cook. I seem to have been the luckiest with Carla the storyteller, juicy apples and a room with a lovely view. But, my energy has suddenly plummeted. I'm feeling rough. I've told Rachel and Jerome about the astrologer's prediction and my looming date, the twenty eighth of March, and the tarot reader's warning of a crisis. They're intrigued and amused.

"No small planes or anything risky on that day!" they joke. Jerome offers me his *mate*.

"Too early in the day for me," I thank him. Too strong, actually.

Chapter 15

SOME LOCAL PEOPLE, including a few shy housewives, a farmer and three lively young children, are also waiting for the bus. Around their feet lie piles of assorted bags and sacks. The farmer, who is craggy-faced, about forty five, wears a black beret, old blue jeans, a black leather jacket and black cowboy boots which come up to his calves. He's trying to keep a tiny, white kitten in a cardboard box and every now and then our eyes meet and we smile. When our driver arrives, Jerome helps the farmer load his gear into the bus. The kitten escapes once again.

I'm very tired but the sense of excitement in reaching my destination and all that it holds in my imagination is huge. Will I find my tribe there? Unfortunately, at this point in time, tiredness—or hangover—has made me forget the advice in the guidebook – **do not bring a suitcase to Tortel**. I heave my overweight wheelie, Shamus, into the back of the bus; we all claim our numbered seats and set off. The journey takes us through more astonishing scenery. Every time we pass an isolated settlement, which consists of a wooden house and outbuildings, our driver slows and hoots his horn and stops. Sometimes he gets out and places a parcel on top of a gatepost, or a rider appears from a forest and collects a sack of something. We drop off locals beside the remotest of homesteads and pick up single passengers in unbelievably far-flung outposts. After about an hour, the road runs beside a wide, flowing river and opposite is a scene which could be a coloured engraving of the pioneer life eighty years ago.

A small rowing boat, painted red, is tied on our side of the river. On the other side is an old, weathered, wooden house surrounded by sheep-pens full of plump sheep. A black horse grazes by the river, the snow-capped Andes rise behind. A dense pine forest lies at the back of the house. This is where our farmer halts the bus. It takes a while to unload the kitten and all the sacks. Every time this wild-looking character passes me with another load of goods, he smiles and his eyes twinkle.

All of a sudden I am fired with the idea to get off the bus here too, in the middle of nowhere and have an adventure. What sort of person would do this? A real adventurer. Yes! Could I do this? I really want to. This is exactly what I was thinking about the other day. Surely this is the next part of my story?

I don't even know the farmer's name. We haven't talked. Just smiled. I want to ask him if he'd rent me a room for a few days, till the next bus passes, for a month, a lifetime? Does he live with his mother? He doesn't look married.

I'm going to have to make a very quick decision. It's still two hours to Tortel and I think the next bus won't come by for a few days. Could I wheel my overweight wheelie down that field, would it sink the boat? No. What would I do for food? What if the next bus didn't come for three days? What if the boat got washed away and I couldn't get back to the road?

Am I brave enough, foolish enough, to jump ship now? This could be a life-changing moment.

AS THE BUS LEAVES in a cloud of dust, Jerome's face stares at me though the back window. I think he's grinning but I'm not sure.

I look down at the opal-coloured river and the dilapidated rowing boat and I feel I'm dreaming. Everything is enchanting and everything unfolds slowly and beautifully. The farmer's name is José and his parents died in an accident when he was nineteen. I'm not sure what the accident was, but he inherited the farm. Then fifteen years ago his wife ran off with his brother. He tells me he loves animals and lives a solitary life, dreaming of sharing it one day with a beautiful foreigner.

The next morning, José makes me breakfast of fried eggs, crispy around the edges, thick buttered bread and black coffee. The eggs have pure orange yolks and the coffee is the most delicious I've ever tasted. José keeps smiling; it's been an incredible night. Sunlight fills the dusty kitchen. Scruffy dogs, skinny cats and fat chickens wander in and out. The new kitten looks lost. And then, suddenly, I am rudely awakened from my wonderful daydream by the driver shouting

"Tortel!"

Tortel?

We have arrived at last at Tortel—and it's raining.

MY EXCITEMENT almost immediately turns into something else. Ashley and Lindsey instantly disappear down one hundred feet of steps to a hostal recommended in the Good Book. Jerome and Rachel make their usual mountain of bags. I'm left with hefty Shamus surveying the scene below. I'd completely forgotten the warning in the guidebook. Now I see why I'm in for trouble. That'll teach me to drink on an empty stomach.

Two little boys try to persuade me to come to their parents' hostal on the other side of the bay. I decline. I want to be right in the middle of Tortel, not looking across the bay at it, but I'm exhausted; it's raining and the village looks about a half mile away, down wooden stepladders and narrow gangplanks. A hill lies in the hazy distance covered with wooden shacks. Behind it lies more of Tortel. How on earth am I going to get Shamus down there, I wonder.

A young couple have watched the bus arrive. They tell me they're Swiss and they're staying at a hostal behind the hill. There are at least three more hostals down there, they say, eyeing me intently. They've arrived by bicycle they add.

The rain gets heavier. I'm having an energy drop at the thought of lugging Shamus up and down those stepladders. Tortel is surrounded by mountains shrouded in grey-green mist. It feels inhospitable and I feel out of place, out of sorts, and a little desperate.

Forty minutes later I've reached the hill and have found a sign saying *comidas*—food. I knock on the door and a grumpy young woman tells me it's past lunch time but she says, she could cook me salmon and chips.

"No thank you," I say. "I just wanted a bowl of soup."

Pause. She looks me up and down.

"I could open a packet of soup," she offers.

"No thank you very much," I say. "Very kind, but no."

No point in launching into an explanation that packet soups, however delicious, will be peppered with additives. These little nasties will set off a string of allergic reactions for me and that will mean I'll be out of action for possibly four days, just if I have one mouthful. I haven't enough energy to explain this. I'm running on empty now.

For the next twenty minutes I get more exhausted as the stepladders get steeper and more slippery. I decide to abandon Shamus and search for a hostal, but when this proves abortive I can't find Shamus. I've become so disoriented I'm completely lost, and one hundred per cent convinced Shamus has been stolen. Is this the warning the astrologer talked about? Is this the crisis? Finally I find Shamus and ten minutes later, after upping and downing more stepladders and gangplanks I arrive at two hostals side by side.

I choose the hostal overlooking the inlet, although the other says *comidas*. I'm ravenous, exhausted and out of sorts. Celia, the owner, shows me around the house and leads me into the kitchen, which is welcoming, cold, old-fashioned but nice. My bedroom is small. It overlooks the pale misty turquoise water. There are two bathrooms. One works, the other doesn't, apparently. Breakfast is at nine, or earlier. It's about three notches up from Neena's. I accept gratefully.

"What about lunch?" I ask.

"No food here," replies Celia.

"Oh, but could you possibly do me just a simple something?" I ask. I think I must look absolutely desperate because she agrees and feeds me upstairs in her own kitchen. My middle-aged, unsmiling landlady generously gives me a three-course meal of delicious leftovers.

Half an hour later I collapse onto my hard, new, single bed. It's going to be my home for the next week or so. I feel like crying. It's weeping outside too. I feel stupid to have brought such an unsuitable case, stupid to have forgotten the warning, and deeply, deeply disappointed and confused that after so much dreaming about this place I feel uncomfortable, foreign and slightly unnerved in a way I can't describe or understand. Something's definitely not right here for me. So without another thought I surrender to sleep. I awake two hours later feeling slightly better, but still way off centre.

> *Random raindrops on the windowpane*
> *Touch them with your fingertip*
> *But there's the barrier of glass*
> *You know that if you wanted*
> *To become involved*
> *You should be*
> *On the other side.*
> *(Anon)*

Chapter 16

WHEN I WAKE UP I feel cold. The view through the window is now almost nil. The sky and sea have merged into a dense, grey, misty mush. I seem to have lost myself somewhere between getting off the bus and getting into bed. What's happened? Nothing's happened! What's triggered this feeling of doom? After all the adventures getting here! Is it the weather? Am I getting ill? Two days to go until the twenty eighth.

By seven in the evening, I've walked to the far end of the village, navigating all the interesting gangplanks and ladders much more easily without Shamus, but I'm drenched again. I'm also dog-tired after so many moves and honestly wishing I'd got off the bus with the farmer and his kitten.

Back in my narrow bedroom, I try to do a bit of a reality check. Why do I want to be anywhere else but here, now that I *am* here? What sort of traveller am I really? What's gone wrong? Am I still looking for more of my story, or have I lost the whole idea? Has it gone as quickly as it arrived, back in January by the lottery kiosk? And what about that hunch that never lets me down? Where's that whispering voice that's been pestering me for a year? Where's my 'teacher' who was supposed to be waiting for me here, or my life lesson? Where's my star gone? I'm not getting it. It's all feeling far too difficult.

I seem to have covered myself with a thick blanket of disappointment. I can't feel anything except disillusion, huge anti-climax and horrible confusion and I've completely lost the ability to see the bigger picture.

A miserable half an hour passes. The hostal is freezing cold. I move myself into the kitchen. The stove's not on yet. With this simple change of scene though, survival mode kicks in, just like a small electric shock. I didn't come all this way to be miserable. I will not give up. It's not an option anyway. What I need to do now is mother myself and I need to be with people. So I put the kettle on the single gas ring and count the remaining herbal tea bags. Twenty! Sitting under the painted cuckoo clock, sipping comforting hot peppermint tea, feeling deeply disorientated, I find myself taking an inventory of the kitchen furniture. I sit still; waiting, looking, wondering who will be the other guests; hoping somebody will come soon.

AFTER A SHORT WHILE, the Swiss couple who watched our bus arrive, open the front door. They turn out to be the only other guests. They're cycling the full length of the Carretera Astral and are on honeymoon. They both speak perfect English. As they prepare their supper—which will be rice and vegetables, enough for three days to take in plastic boxes in the bike panniers—Claudia tells me their story of arriving in Tortel by bus. Chopping mushrooms, she begins her tale.

"When we drove down from Cochrane yesterday, the driver seemed to stop at every single settlement. He hooted his horn. Guess he was hoping a passenger would emerge. It was taking ages. When we approached the Rio Baker, a middle-aged local guy on the bus got very excited and ran down the aisle to the driver, it was a long bus. He insisted we stopped. The two men then leapt out and ran like a pair of kids down to the river's edge. They picked up stones and started throwing them wildly into the water. Suddenly they took off their shoes and socks and waded in up to their knees. A few minutes later the bus was chugging down the dirt track highway again with a fat salmon lying in the aisle. The passenger and the driver were grinning and chatting. Somebody was in for a great supper that night."

Our landlady finally arrives and by nine o'clock the stove is going and the kitchen is cosy. The cooking facilities are practically zilch—no cooking pots—but the stove is roaring, a kettle's boiling and stale breakfast bread becomes hot toast. I eat my last emergency meal—a flapjack and some dried fruit.

THE RAIN IS LIGHTER the next morning. I set off to do another recce of the village and meet Ashley and Lindsey. They're trying to find a boatman to take them to the Isla de Los Muertos, the island nearby where one hundred immigrant workers died in mysterious circumstances.

"Would you like to come too? The more people the cheaper the price," they say.

I'm a little ambivalent but agree, so we set off together to find a boatman who will to take us tomorrow, which just happens to be the twenty eighth of March. I've decided to ignore the astrologer's warning.

Ashley and Lindsey are preoccupied with their travel arrangements for getting out of Tortel the day after tomorrow. They have a complicated, ambitious and arduous itinerary ahead. They're heading for Argentina. To get there from here, they first have to hook up with a bus at the crossroads twenty five kilometres from Tortel. If they miss it, they'll have to wait four days for the next one. If they catch the bus, after a two hour journey, they'll then need to find the small boat—only one a week now—to cross Lake O'Higgins, which is dotted with icebergs. Next, they have to hire two horses and find a guide. It will be a two day ride into Argentina. Rachel and Jerome are also going the same route, but they don't seem concerned about the time factor or all the arrangements. Ashley and Lindsey are in danger of not seeing Tortel because of these preoccupations and I am in danger of not seeing Tortel because of this all-pervasive cloud of fatigue and disappointment. I feel like a spoilt child who's had too many birthday presents all at once and I hate feeling like this.

My four new friends are staying at a Neena-style hostal with a cranky landlady. It's near the entrance to the village and is only just OK, they say. I have inadvertently chosen the recommended hostal from The Bible. Rachel and Jerome have found somewhere else right at the far end of the village where they can cook.

"We'll move tomorrow," says Rachel, when I bump into them later. "Tortel is absolutely wonderful," she enthuses. "You must be in your element here, Meg. It's fabulous. We absolutely love it. It's so mysterious, so different, so interesting. The boardwalks are amazing; we think we might live here for a while. You too?"

I feel envious they are having the experience which I'd anticipated.

"Getting very near the twenty eighth!" teases Jerome.

I tell them I've decided to ignore the astrologer's warning and that I'm going to the Island of the Dead with the others tomorrow, in a boat.

"You want to come too?" I ask.

They look at each other and fall about laughing.

"You are going on a boat to the Island of the Dead on the fated twenty eighth?"

They're winding me up. After more teasing I gradually manage to change the subject. It feels a bit like juggling balls in the air. I let the twenty eighth fall on the floor and disappear and then I tell them about my film and how they've inspired me. Jerome sips his *mate* and smiles. He stares knowingly into the far distance. His expression becomes sad, then blank; then he smiles again.

"Let's keep in touch," he says. "The film sounds great."

Rachel touches my arm and beams. Our friendship is somehow sealed. The film feels born and approved. After agreeing to hire a boat together, we go our separate ways. I decide to have lunch in the tiny, three-table restaurant on stilts called El Mirador.

Salmon and chips is what's on offer and it's served by friendly Anna Marie. Her three young children, all wearing Scottish kilts, play in the restaurant. Her serious husband, Hector, is painting a newly built-on room which will give them space for four more tables. Their little wooden house with the kitchen below is in a spectacular location. It looks right out into the fjord.

The sky is getting clearer by the hour and the grey-green water is slowly turning to opal. Anna Marie answers my questions about Prince William and Rosie Swale, the intrepid solo explorer who ended her epic horseback ride down through South America here. Anna Marie doesn't remember her, but she remembers Prince William well.

"He passed by here every day at twelve on the dot!" she tells me. "He'd be on his way to buy a bag of chips! He liked chips! He told me once he loved Tortel because it was the only place in the world where he'd ever felt like an ordinary human being."

She goes on to explain that William was here with Operation Raleigh, an international youth project set up by his father.

"The group of teenagers were here for three months to repair the gang planks and make new ones. They lived on the ship in the bay over there. I don't know where they went after here."

Anna Marie persuades me to try her home-made cake. It has three layers of mouth-watering butterscotch and cream. Then she tells me about other artists and writers who have come and made temporary homes in Tortel, like the French photographer Sophie who's published a book of photos of the villagers.

MY LANDLADY has left for Coyhaique for a week and the Swiss couple have also moved on. So when I return to base, I meet shy Señor Renaldo, aged about forty two, a little overweight and on crutches.

"I'm going to be deputising for your landlady," he explains quietly.

He's got the stove roaring and has a slightly shy expression. Renaldo is recovering from a serious operation on his leg and hobbles about Tortel on crutches. Poor man – all those ladders and all those steps. He's got a huge chuck of bloody meat wedged into a pan and he asks me if I'd like to have lunch with him.

"I've already eaten," I thank him sincerely.

Renaldo turns out to be an endless, generous, gentle font of local information. He loves Tortel with a passion. He tells me the new president Michelle Bachelet has visited the village.

Ashley and Lindsey drop in after lunch. I offer them herbal tea and it's lovely to feel at home with them in our friendly, now cosy, kitchen with its wonderful views of the azure inlet. The sun's now popping in and out. Colours are appearing and disappearing. Renaldo's back at work. His meat bone is still stewing in the pot. My new friends still haven't sorted out their getaway plan.

After our tea, they take me to the village supermarket close to the office where we have to register our names for the boat trip tomorrow. The coastguard asks us for our passport numbers (in case we drown?) and the thought of hiking back to the hostal to find mine makes me lie.

"Passport number, Señora?" he asks me.

Ashley and Lindsey know theirs off by heart. I invent a number, and as I do so, a little dart of panic shoots though my head.

On our way back to my hostal we pass the tiny restaurant on stilts and meet Anna Marie and Hector. He's still painting, the kids are still playing. Ashley asks me to ask him if he can shed any light on their transport conundrum, and in no time at all he's come up with the perfect plan. His friend works at the junction of the road, where the bus will stop briefly at eleven o'clock. What transpires is that Hector's friend will take their backpacks at seven, and they will hike the twenty five kilometres to the crossroads, in time to catch eleven o'clock bus. They are super-fit, brave adventurers and they like to hike.

IN THE EARLY EVENING Rachel and Jerome come to visit me. I offer them herbal tea and we sink into the elderly, comfy sofas like old friends. Renaldo is out when a middle-aged German couple arrive. I show them the Swiss couple's room and they decide to take it. They've wisely left their backpacks in their car. They return forty minutes later—puffing a little—to meet Renaldo and become part of this transient family. The house is now wonderfully cosy. Our host likes food and likes to be warm. He also loves loud TV.

Tomorrow at eleven we'll meet up with our boatman, Pedro, at the jetty beside the roundhouse library on stilts. It'll be a twenty minute journey to the island. Sabine, the German woman, has decided to join us. Her handsome husband Peter has signed up for the challenging eleven hour expedition to the vast southern ice field, the Ventisquero.

Chapter 17

THE NEXT MORNING, MARCH THE TWENTY EIGHTH, the sun is almost shining and the deep autumn colours of Tortel show themselves. We meet Pedro as arranged. He hands out life vests. I'm worrying about having given a false passport number. I can hear my thirty eight year old son's voice clearly in my head.

"That was a bl**dy stupid, irresponsible thing to do Mother!"

"I know. I agree."

"So, why didn't you bring it the next morning?"

"I forgot. Too busy thinking about thermal underwear and breakfast!"

I cringe. How could I be so forgetful? Easily it seems.

THE OUTBOARD MOTOR springs into action and we splash fast though grey-green water, mountains soaring on either side. We pass many small uninhabited islands. Ashley sits in the bow catching the strong spray in her face. She beams. Very soon I feel like I've got a bag of frozen peas stuck to my forehead; the freezing wind bites deep and our small boat crashes up and down though waves washed in from the Pacific Ocean. The vast northern and southern ice fields lie just hours in front and behind us. Antarctica is just a few hours away by plane. We get soaked with spray in minutes. Luckily I brought all my Alaskan thermal gear, but forgot the hat. Just as my head feels like its going to split with the cold, Rachel taps me on my shoulder and mimes would I like her woolly cap. She pulls the collar of her black fleece over her own head and smiles.

Ten minutes later Pedro turns the engine off and we glide into a calm lagoon. He docks the boat and we clamber onto a marshy bank. Yet another wooden walkway takes us to an information board where we read the history of the Island of the Dead:

"Over a hundred men women and children died here in mysterious circumstances in 1901."

We read the information slowly, respectfully, silently.

"Immigrant workers hired by an Englishman arrive in boatloads from the poverty stricken island of Chiloé. Their mission was to clear the land, plant crops, and make a community."

Some stories say they all died because deadly mice droppings contaminated their food supplies. That's how Lena's pioneer father died in Puyuhuapi. Other stories say the ruthless English landlord poisoned his workers—many of whom were Irish—rather than pay them for a year's work. Whatever happened, over one hundred men, women and children died right here.

In a small copse of holly oaks, there remain thirty or forty wooden crosses marking their graves. Only two still have names just legible, but they've been re-written for visitors' benefit Pedro tells us later. A few years ago three skeletons were exhumed, and after extensive forensic tests, the university professors found nothing but silence and more mystery.

In single file, slowly—almost ceremonially—we walk the gangplank towards the graves and a sense of immense peace fills my whole being. To our right there's a vast expanse of marshland, alive with swaying grasses growing around a pale green lagoon. In the middle distance sits a range of purple mountains. In the far distance the mighty Andes tower paler purple. As we approach the graves, I experience a sense of déjà vu.

The weathered, wooden crosses covered with moss and silvery lichen are staked at angles, some pointing slightly west, others east. They're surrounded by thick, deep-green ferns. There's a primitive wooden fence preventing people from going too near; no touching allowed.

If this scene was part of my movie, the accompanying music would be exquisite – a kind of homecoming, a prodigal son/daughter theme, a wide angle shot, a kind of 'Ahhha! At last I'm home—' … and it's March twenty eighth! If I were Shirley Maclaine, the actress/mystic, I would be telling you I feel myself here as a young woman. I sense myself clearing the land. There's an adoring young husband standing smiling beside me. I'm blissfully happy with my new life spreading out in front of me. I have a baby girl strapped to my back. I'm a *campesina,* a peasant, with a precious, loving family. An Irish immigrant with a beautiful dream.

I'm looking at the marshlands now. I know this place. I've been here before.

DURING THE BOAT JOURNEY BACK to Tortel, nobody says a word. I find myself in a kind of altered state. The beauty and the tragedy of the island intermingle in every part of my being and I sink into a profound silence. The water is calm now. Greeny-blue. Flat.

BACK AT THE HOSTAL, IN MY SMALL BEDROOM with its two single side-by-side beds, I try to take stock. Surprisingly, the island experience fades quickly, like a dream beckoned back into the night, but it leaves its trace; an imprint on my soul. Is what has just happened linked to those whispering feelings, those inner knowings I couldn't argue with, which drew me here in the first place? Is this why I came here? And if so, who or where is the 'teacher' I thought I'd find here? What's the life lesson I'm supposed to learn from this experience?

Then, unexpectedly, as evening quietly arrives—like fast forwarding a film—I find myself thrust once again into horrible depression. I'm glued back into those black feelings, that awful alienation from myself and the world that makes me feel so wretched. It doesn't happen often these days, but it's happening now.

Many months later, insights about the island experience arrive in three separate 'instalments'. But now in my chilly bedroom, without the benefit of any hindsight or insight, I'm trying to reverse this unnerving feeling that occasionally invades my body, mind and spirit. How can all that anticipation, curiosity and excitement about Tortel turn so sour so quickly? It's a bit like I read the wrong page in the guidebook. This isn't the Tortel I imagined.

Tomorrow's Sunday, I think I'll leave on Monday. I'm out of my depth here. I feel horrible—unwelcome—despite my mystical experience.

FUNNY THOUGH, WITH HINDSIGHT, how geographically I got it right. The location, I mean. The bull's-eye, so to speak. It seems it was for the reverse reason I came all the way to Tortel – not to find a new story and a new home, but to remember an old one. Past lives? Yes, past lives. I can see my sons' eyebrows disappearing under their hairlines.

How extraordinary to have been magnetically pulled right down through Patagonia, down the bumpy spine of the magnificent Andes—to where I thought my film story and new life might be—to believe I've been here before.

Could this be the setting for my film? Could I transport Rachel and Jerome back in time to an island which cradled over a hundred dreams to the grave?

TORTEL IS A LABYRINTH of narrow boardwalks and little wooden houses hugging the mountainside. It's a mysterious, intensely beautiful dramatic location. But it's like a close-kept secret not wanting to be discovered. It is home to a collection of fiercely independent people. The women I pass on the gangplanks seem shy and wary. The men—mostly loggers or fishermen—are lean and weathered. Men's men. From a distance I've watched these loggers sprinting up the steep stepladders, racing along the gang planks, balancing heavy bundles of roughly cut Cypruses on their shoulders. Once a month they load their motor boats with the wood and rendezvous at the mouth of the inlet with a cargo boat. The wood is shipped to Argentina to make fence posts. This is a main source of income for the village. These brave, pioneering people seem unaccustomed to visitors. It feels like their secret's been told by mistake and they rue the day their village was discovered.

I've sunk so low despite the island experience, much of the time I've forgotten why I came here.

Hindsight tells me if I'd stayed for a month, I'd be telling you a different story. And just the next day an opportunity presents itself to open doors for me in the village. But today, this is one of those crossroads in life. Each new decision brings a series of different experiences, and who's to say what's best at the end of the day?

THE SKY IS HEAVY WITH CLOUD, the village is quiet. I pull myself out of my small bedroom and go for a walk. Navigating more slippery gangplanks and the steep stepladders, taking care not to fall, I find a wooden bench at the far end of the village, sit down and rest in the gentle, comforting sounds of water and the creaking of two old rowing-boats tied to a jetty. It's early evening. Where will I go next? What will I do now?

One part of my three-fold 'mission' to Patagonia has been accomplished. I finally got to Tortel. But the central objective of the trip is far from finished. The two main characters and the magical, mysterious feel of the film story have been birthed, but there's still so much more to be unearthed. And I haven't found my new winter home yet— though I'm discovering that my southern American tribe are my fellow world travellers—school teacher Marta and café owner Lorinda being the exceptions.

I could go south now to Tierra Del Fuego—gateway to Antarctica—that small chunk of land at the very end of the world; a place of magnificent sunsets and thousands of penguin colonies; or east into Argentina, a country with a heartbreaking history and a passion for dance; or north, back to the historic city of Santiago with its tarot readers, street markets and vibrant art scene. West from here lies the Pacific Ocean, with hundreds of shipwrecked dreams and rich treasures lying mute on its underworld bed. Could more of my film story be wedged into any of these alluring locations? I really don't know, but intuitively I think not.

So I wait—delayed by an inner fog—gazing onto the azure inlet, allowing time for that wee small voice to make itself known again. Despite everything that appears to have gone pear-shaped in the last few days—somehow, in these lost moments, a little bit of me still *knows* I'll be drawn by my star.

SITTING BY THE WATERSIDE, FEELING BLANK, feeling damp, hoping to see a dolphin or a condor, gradually, slowly, some inexplicable process begins to take place in my heart and silently, without words, a shift happens. Andres, the gentle Canadian wilderness guide comes into my mind like a haunting poster for a missing person, posted everywhere I look. This wildly mysterious man holds a huge attraction and a secret story. *Yes, I know he's married,* but this is nothing to do with romance. It's something else. What *is* his secret? Is it linked in some way to the success of my film? Will I meet somebody through him who will fall in love with the concept of the movie and want to produce it, buy it? I don't think so. I haven't refined the concept yet. All of a sudden I'm exploding inside with curiosity. Without any personal expectations or desires, I 'know' the pull to this man is something to do with love. Could it be to do with the blissful love I glimpsed on the island? Is *he* living this bliss? Will I see *it* in action? Or has he lost his bliss? Have we known each other before? Is he some kind of archetypal teacher?

Like waking up from a dream with a jolt, I suddenly feel my inner compass swinging north towards Andres in Chaiten. That's where I'll go next. I'll arrive by boat! I'll catch the repaired ferry at Coyhaique. Surely it'll be fixed by now? And if not, I'll return by the dirt track highway, the famous, fabulous Carretera Austral, travelling by a string of those characterful little unpredictable minibuses.

I leave the bench overlooking the harbour and head for the hostal, an enormous smile illuminating my whole being. Out of thin air, so to speak, a brand new agenda has arrived. It's another of those unrelenting tugs at the heart. It's the invisible thread pulling again. And it's the voiceless voice once more.

Walking slowly back along the gangplanks I remember that in Coyhaique, half way to Andres, there's a Spanish language school run by a foreigner. Maybe I could break the journey there for a few days and take some Spanish lessons? Also in Coyhaique, there's Javier the talented stone carver. Maybe they could both give me lessons? I will not under any circumstances be returning to Hostal Neena, even though it's just possible I may give her a bit part in my film.

BY THE TIME I'M BACK IN THE KITCHEN, the lovely inner smile has turned into a fiery surge of new energy cancelling out all the darkness of the past few days. In a funny kind of a way, I imagine this is the energy that propelled people over generations to prospect for gold. And I'm guessing it's the same kind of insatiable curiosity that led ancient mariners on impossible journeys. But *my* goal is not about acquiring earthly treasures, or 'acquiring' a person. It's about being pulled by my star again. Hindsight tells me I'm being pulled to learn more about the treasure of what love really is. Many adopted people find this profoundly confusing. I sense I got it right in that past life, but I'm not getting it right in this. What I witnessed on the beach in front of the turquoise lake, when Rachel and Jerome danced and set my imagination on fire, is—is what I don't have, it's what is missing in my life today. The dance of partnership. I sense Andres holds this key.

So, my heart, which has a mind of its own, has decided on a new route. *Nothing* else in the world interests me right now. I'll travel north by sea. Surely the ferry will be fixed?

My mind jumps to Chaiten. I'll spend more time in the beautiful Casa Redonda and I'll take the hike in the rain forest again, this time with Andres. What might happen if you put two secretive people together in a lush rain forest glistening with fungus, freak-coloured moss and God knows what else, make them clamber though steep trails seething with wildlife, have them wade up streams over moss-carpeted and lichen-covered logs, tight-roping over makeshift bridges for twelve hours? Might one crack? Change? Tell all?

When I piece together the small amount of information I have about Andres, it feels like this enigmatic person is acting out some key part in a contemporary—yet ancient—South American folk tale or legend. Or is it a *universal* tale? People love him. He loves people. He's a good, kind, man. He's charismatic, and /but, he's got a fascinating personality 'flaw'. He's elusive.

Andres does indeed turn out to be a major key-holder in my journey, my film and my life—but not in a way I could ever have guessed.

Chapter 18

SUNDAY MORNING DAWNS CLEAR and Tortel is beginning to look different. I decide to visit the local church. Renaldo tells me mass starts at ten thirty. I'm quite unprepared for what follows.

The church is a fine, wooden building and outside it sits a life-sized statue of Father Guiseppi, lovingly carved by a local young man from an enormous Cyprus trunk. This Italian priest—who brought the animals in a boat to the starving families of Tortel in 1955 and saved them from certain death—is a local hero.

Opening the church door, I'm greeted by a friendly middle aged woman who excitedly explains something to me I don't fully understand. She pulls me out of the church, still smiling and talking fast. I comply and find myself following her into another wooden building close by.

Miriam opens the door and I'm surprised to find we're inside a sophisticated recording studio.

"Sit down, sit down," she says pointing to a chair.

She sits opposite me behind a huge deck of controls. Easy Listening music is already playing in the background. Miriam picks up the microphone, turns down the sound and says boldly:

"Good morning Tortel. *Grandes cosas hizo el Señor por nosotros,*"—"great things the Lord has done for us".

"This morning we have an Irish artist visiting us from Spain. She'd like to say a few words to you about herself and how she finds Tortel."

Miriam thrusts the mike into my hand and waits with eyebrows raised.

"Oh," I say. "Oh. Aaaaah, *buenos días a todo—*"

I keep my response short. Miriam beams when I hand back the mike. She turns up the music and beckons me to follow her back into the church. New-agey music will now be piped into the homes of Tortel for the next half hour. This is the Sunday service.

Back in the church, we stand in front of the altar and Miriam lights a candle. It's the first time I've been the only person at a mass. I'm given a folded pamphlet which is headed *El Domingo día Del Señor*—Sunday day of our Lord. Miriam says a short prayer then asks me to read from the pamphlet.

"Sorry," I say. "But I can't read very well in Spanish. I read like a five year old!"

"Never mind," she says, at which point we are joined by Aurelia, who has thick black hair down to her waist, is about thirty and wears a longish, black, leather jacket. She looks like she might have parked her Harley Davidson nearby, except that's not possible in Tortel.

"Read," says Miriam, thrusting another pamphlet into Aurelia's hand. She lights a second candle.

From then on Aurelia reads the long passages, Miriam the short. I am amazed to hear Miriam read. She sounds just like me but with a better accent. It's touching and humbling. When finally I'm asked to read the closing prayer I don't mind. But before that something poignant and unexpected happens.

We've just got to the point in the mass where we to turn to the person beside us and 'give the peace', a peck on each cheek or a handshake if it's a stranger. The door of the church bursts opens just as Miriam says: "And now give the peace—"

In rushes—staggers—an elderly man. He looks biblical from the head down. He's dazed and shaking, white hair flowing over his shoulders, long beard touching his thin chest. His trainers and coat are well worn and old. He stops right in front of Miriam. His mouth opens and he looks wild. I wonder how she's going to cope with this.

She walks a step forward and kisses him, and then he turns to me and gives me the softest kiss on both cheeks. Then he kisses Aurelia and stumbles a few paces backwards, looking stunned as though just caught in the beam of car headlights.

"Now read the last prayer, Margarita," Miriam commands.

Afterwards, there's no coffee in the crypt—no crypt or vestry—but Miriam fills me in on a little of the background to the church. First I discover our elderly, long-haired gentleman is a resident of the village, possibly the oldest. He has Parkinson's disease and is cared for by women employed by the town hall. When there's a tragedy in the village the church is full, Miriam tells me.

I walk slowly home to Renaldo, who is having leftover meaty goat bone for lunch.

AFTER EATING SOME SALAD AND APPLES I trek along the gangplank to find Rachel and Jerome's new home. It's right at the far end of the village, the views are spectacular. The young couple are thrilled with it.

I find them in the kitchen looking at a large, square book of black and white photos of Tortel and its inhabitants. The photographer is a youngish French woman from Paris who lives in the village for spells every year. Anna Marie at the restaurant has told me about her. The photos are incredible, but they epitomise all the sense of exclusion and fear I have about this place. Turning page after page I think I'm in a surreal movie where I've just dropped in from another planet, another reality, another dimension. And in a sense I have. This is not my world, I don't feel welcome here. Nothing is familiar. Many of the characters are laughing at the camera. A flood of strange, old, uncomfortable feelings surge though me. Not welcome. Go away. Keep away. Aram-Aitch's message.

"Amazing, eh?" says Jerome.

"Incredible," sighs Rachel. The landlady adds that we can buy a copy of the book at the roundhouse library for thirty euros.

THE IMPACT OF THE PHOTOGRAPHS sticks all over me like Clingfilm for the rest of the day and I remember again the power of art; the power an image has to communicate and trigger emotions. In order to capture so many extraordinary portraits—these are no snapshots—the artist-photographer has developed a special relationship with these people. She's also needed tremendous technical skill. I study the small photo of the wild-haired photographer on the book jacket and decide she would fit in well here. She would not have arrived with a heavy wheelie and a zip-lock bag full of assorted herbal tea bags. But she would have come with a dream too, pulled by her star, for sure. A special breed. An intrepid traveller. The sort of person who would get off a bus in the middle of nowhere with a farmer and a kitten, and stay.

BACK IN MY HOSTAL I share another herbal tea—not many left now—with Sabine, the German woman who came with us to the Isla de los Muertos. She tells me her husband Peter is an architect. We swap travel stories and Sabine tells me she prefers Asia to Chile. She smiles a lot.

Rachel and Jerome visit later in the evening. It's lovely to sit around the kitchen stove feeling so at home with these interesting strangers. The young French couple have decided to skip the route to Argentina via the boat and horse trek route. We speculate whether Ashley and Lindsey made it to the crossroads; whether they caught the last boat of the season; whether they found the horses and the guide. Did they make the arduous two-day trek into Argentina? I picture them trudging over green scrub in the rain, ambling over hills and through thick forests by moonlight, fading into a purple distance on tired horses, *Lonely Planet* Bible safely tucked into a large saddlebag.

During the early evening Renaldo finishes his goat stew, so I manage to use his pan to make some ratatouille. Whilst cooking my vegetable stew, Sabine invites me to join them in their hired four-by-four. They're heading north tomorrow. Would I like to come with them? This idea popped into my mind earlier, so I accept graciously, but not too quickly and we agree to leave early tomorrow morning for Cochrane.

I'm heading for pretty, Austrian-looking, Puerto Anand, a tiny village north of Cochrane. Our bus stopped there briefly on the way down to Tortel. It's a collection of colourful, interesting, small, painted wooden houses beside a turquoise lake, lots of flowers in yards, but unlike neat and tidy Austria, this place had a wildness I loved. A foreigner in his garden had shouted something with a strong accent to our friendly bus driver. I noticed a mural of a volcano and a rushing river painted on the side of his house and a stack of kayaks lying upturned in his wild garden. Later somebody told me he was a wilderness and kayak guide, a friend of Marta's in Futaleufú and of Gabor and Andres in Chaiten. He is known as Daniel, the quiet American, another legend in the making, apparently.

THE THOUGHT OF LUGGING SHAMUS back to the car park above the village, up all those stepladders and steep steps fills me with dread. I really wanted to arrive in Tortel by boat, like everybody did until three years ago when the road was built, but it proved too complicated and too expensive. Leaving by boat has also proved too expensive and too complicated. But one option has presented itself. Sitting on a raft made of a pile of tree trunks, with a couple of guys paddling, would be affordable. This is a possibility. But I decide that might not be such a good idea. The crisis is still to happen and I hear an echo of my own voice, as though calling from the other end of a long tunnel—"Don't do it!" I feel a second-class traveller, though, for not having the persistence and energy to try this adventure.

THE NEXT MORNING when I emerge from our hostal wheeling Shamus, Renaldo greets me warmly on the deck, but his smile disappears as our eyes both drift down to my suitcase on little wheels.

"You want some help with that?" he asks kindly.

"Yes," I say. "PLEASE." Renaldo puts two fingers to his mouth, whistles loudly and in minutes a small man appears form the jetty below.

"He'll take you in his boat round the bay, save you climbing a lot of ladders," Renaldo says. "Agree a price first, about five pesos."

I can't believe my luck. Marco heaves Shamus onto his shoulder and we descend the two hundred or so slippery muddy steps to the waterside, where I struggle to get onto his low wooden boat.

We whiz across the bay and I'm ecstatic—ecstatic I'm getting help, ecstatic I'm leaving, ecstatic I've made it here, ecstatic I'm feeling connected, plugged in again. On the jetty, another four hundred wet steps loom above us. Oh God, I'm thinking, just as Marco asks if I want him to carry Shamus up there too.

"Oh yes," I say. "Please. Thank you." And off he sprints like a mountain hare. At the top I feel slightly stunned that something which I thought was going to be so hard turns out to be so easy. Once again I get exactly what I need, rather than what I want on this trip. That's what I mean by being plugged in, connected and looked after—drawn by a star.

Part 2

The Road to Andres

Chapter 19

THE DRIVE TO PUERTO ANAND in a four-by-four is a new experience. It's luxurious after all the battered little minibuses. It feels like I'm starting a completely new adventure; a whole fresh scenario is about to unfold. Destination Chaiten. Mission: to find the real Andres. And if I'm truthful—which I hardly dare be—I want to discover why I'm so attracted to this man. But I'm also still on the hunt for my new home and I'm still searching for more characters, sub-themes and interesting challenges for my movie. The adventure is by no means over yet. I have a feeling *something big* is just around the corner.

The back seat of the jeep is piled high with expensive German backpacks, so the left view—towards the Andes and the river—is nil. Everything slides onto the floor as we speed out of Tortel. Athletic, fifty eight year old Bavarian Peter stops the vehicle, jumps out, restacks and pummels the mound of rucksacks. Then in real Boy Scout fashion, he ties a length of string out of the window, over the roof rack and onto the door handle.

"Fine now," he says and grins. Except that I still can't see a thing.

It's wonderful to be able to stop wherever we want, so we stop frequently. We're not in a hurry. The day is bright and sunny and the three of us are all in great spirits. Awesome waterfalls, herds of wild horses, interesting rope bridges, fabulous colours, bottled water, are all shared with delight.

Then we come to Cochrane again, scene of Lindsey's birthday dinner, Hospedaje Juanjo, Carla and the farmer and the kitten at the bus stop.

"We know a great place to buy the very best *empanadas* here," says Peter, sweeping round corners trying to find the supermarket where they feasted on these pasties and fabulous German cakes. At times, Peter drives like a competitive rally driver.

Empanadas are pasties filled with meat, olives and chopped hard boiled eggs. They are either in pastry parcels or, better still, battered in deep-fried little packets. We buy both sorts. And the cakes. Oh bliss! Black Forest gateau, cheesecake, chocolate fudge cake. We stock up and start the search for a picnic place.

ARRIVING IN PUERTO ANAND, we stop outside a pretty, three-storey, wooden hostal. Below the hostal, on the ground floor, is the village store. The middle-aged female owner, snugly attired in a hand-knitted, sludge-coloured cardigan, tells me curtly that the hostal is closed for the season.

"I'm alone now, so how can I possibly run a guest house and a shop?" she demands.

A glass-fronted showcase in a dark corner of the shop is full of hand-knitted brown scarves and small crocheted coffee coloured hats. I buy a hat because it's just like the one I used in my smuggling days in East Berlin. How extraordinary to have that memory triggered. The shelves of the village store are lined with tinned fruit and bright-coloured sweeties.

"There are a few other hostals in the village," the tired owner volunteers crustily.

The sunny day has changed. It's grey now. The village is not at all as Austrian-looking as I remembered, but it's still enchanting. We drive up a hill above the lake and pass a wooden cabin. A roadside sign says *'Welcome',* but Peter continues driving until we come to The Blue House Hostal. It looks tiny. We couldn't all possibly fit it there, surely? It's a doll's house. Further up there's a sign for a fishing lodge.

"That'll be expensive," Sabine decides.

We return to the first log cabin overlooking the river, and I ask the owner if they are open.

ABRAHÁN—a tall, slim, elderly gentleman with a slight stoop—says yes, they have rooms, but they're not quite ready. There's a smell of fresh paint, and the unmade beds are piled high with blankets.

"Come back in fifteen minutes," he says, "we'll be ready for you then. And would you like supper tonight? I can cook you something."

Peter and Sabine return in five minutes, I linger a bit longer.

My room, with two single beds, is in the attic. It has a view of the turquoise river through ancient eucalyptus trees. Chickens and dogs wander leisurely around the garden below. Peter and Sabine have the downstairs en-suite room. They're happy with it.

Abrahán, a gentle six-foot-something retired farmer, owns the hostal. His son Carlito and shy daughter-in-law Lorena help him run it. They live nearby in another wooden cabin they've built themselves. Later, Abrahán shows me a third cabin amongst the pine trees, also overlooking the lake. I'm thinking this could be it—this could be my home for next winter. I love the village. It's pretty and wild and right beside the lake and the mouth of the River Baker. But I'd need to find somewhere else to paint. There's no room for mess in this little elf's house. Abrahán smiles.

"Think about it and let me know when you decide," he says.

Peter and Sabine go for a walk. I see them sitting on a small jetty beside the lake, talking. It's an intimate scene and I wonder what they're talking about. It transpires she's the mayor of her town in Germany. She's just been re-elected for the third time. Sabine doesn't say much but she listens attentively. I find this fascinating for a successful politician. Maybe that's her secret. They planned this trip to start right after the election, so if she won—fine—and if she didn't—fine too, they'd go to South America anyway. But Sabine isn't in love with Chile as I am. Puerto Anand has awoken this passion again.

AT SEVEN O'CLOCK we sit down to a delicious supper of chicken stew and vegetables. Abrahán, Carlito and Lorena sit at a table beside us. Sabine and Peter don't speak Spanish, so I find myself in the role of translator once again. I don't mind. They ask masses of intelligent questions.

Abrahán clears the table and returns with three small porcelain bowls full of tinned strawberries topped with tinned cream. It feels such a treat.

"I used to have animals here," he tells us. "Everything was fresh then—milk, butter, cream. But I sold all the animals ten years ago. I've been baking bread every day since."

He smiles again.

"We built all the cabins here ourselves and we've had guests coming from far and wide."

There are photos of him on the walls—scenes with jovial fishermen, arms linked, large fish at their feet. He towers above most of his guests; lean, weathered, a kind face, a kind soul. Somebody you could trust with your life, in a small boat on a rough lake if need be.

The next morning Peter and Sabine decide to leave and invite me to join them again. As I think I may have found where I will come back to next winter, I decline and explain.

AFTER BREAKFAST Abrahán suggests that Carlito takes me to a local beauty spot. It's where two rivers converge and make beautiful waterfalls. We set off in his white van and he tells me he used to have a boat business nearby. Something went wrong and they had to sell up and move. He doesn't explain, but his facial grimaces tell me it was a traumatic experience.

We park the van and I'm interested to discover he isn't sure how to get to these waterfalls. We seem to be following rabbit trails. Finally we arrive and the scene is magnificent. Behind the rivers rise two awe-inspiring mountains. I scan the peaks with my binoculars. The melting snow reveals dramatic shapes under both summits. There are black gulleys like deep wounds, grey scratches like fine veins and indented, grey snow-recesses where perhaps a huge body fell. Stretching the imagination a little more, some marks look like yeti footprints. It's a wonderful, unforgettable, magical, National Geographic moment. I hand the binoculars to Carlito. He scours the mountains and smiles. He doesn't often smile. He's entranced too. Suddenly I'm completely surprised to see a young woman standing on a rock twenty feet downstream. How did she get there? Then a group of about eight young adults appear. Their guide, seeing Carlito, greets his friend warmly. The party have come down from Coyhaique for the day. I offer my binoculars to the other guide. He too scans the high peaks and smiles. How sweet these shared moments when words aren't necessary.

The way back is easy. We arrived following rabbit tracks and leave following a well-trodden horse trail. Small mounds of old dry horse dung punctuate the track as we push our way through waist-high gorse bushes. When we get home, Abrahán announces lunch is ready.

ABRAHÁN AND I eat alone. He's prepared a feast. First there's a soupy stew which he slurps with gusto. I'm tempted to giggle and slurp too. There are home-made bread rolls and butter, then a second course of pasta coated in tomato puree, nice and gooey with parmesan cheese. It's completely stuck to the pot. Then there are more strawberries and cream, followed by coffee and a wrapped chocolate. I'm experiencing a strong feeling I can't quite describe. Maybe it's *tenderness, or softness, or warmth*. Whatever it is, I know this is a precious moment in time.

Abrahán suggests that if I really have to leave tomorrow, Carlito should take me to find a boatman who'll show me the extraordinary place in the lake where the two different coloured lakes meet, but the two colours don't merge. I agree enthusiastically. Then follows a long siesta.

At five o'clock that afternoon, there's no sign of either Abrahán or Carlito and I am wondering if I've misunderstood the arrangement about the boat adventure.

By half past five, father and son return, subdued after a heated community meeting at the village hall. Carlito is instructed to take me to a nearby fishing lodge to find a man who will take me out in his boat, for a fee. How much it will be I ask.

"How much is it worth to you?" he replies.

THE FIFTEEN PESOS JOURNEY down the lake is unforgettable. Paco, the boatman, is a new father with a tiny baby who doesn't sleep much. He's silent and so am I. It's getting to sunset time. The water is turquoise on one side of the boat, grey-blue on the other. Close to Puerto Anand where the two lakes merge to become a river, the colours eventually join and become the famous turquoise Rio Baker which flows down to Tortel, and out into the Pacific Ocean.

Paco switches off the engine and our boat glides gently into the astonishing line where turquoise meets steely-blue, but both refuse to marry. Argentina is on the other side of the lake, Chile behind and all around us. I want to go further, stay longer, savour more. But without a word, the engine springs to life and Paco heads back home for more family life.

AFTER THE BOAT ADVENTURE, I sit on a log beside the lake and watch the sun set.

I've collected many short stories so far and many characters. I allow them to make their presence felt again. Like actors auditioning, they come on the stage of my mind's eye—or my heart's mind—and mime a coded message:

First there's the opera singer with the angelic voice from the dingy tunnel, the busker full of promise. She gets stage fright, can't sing, looks terrified, no eye contact. Something awful must have happened to her, she seems unable to smile. Her name is Sasha.

Then there's Anton, the mysterious, possibly Russian, tarot reader who warns of a crisis. He waves a swirling red flag as he bends double to take a bow. He's a messenger of some sort.

Then there's Babette, the artist owner of the lavender farm, she's being theatrical, doing the can-can, till she stumbles and falls. Is she a trickster?

Marta has to be coaxed to audition – she's dragged on stage by fifty little five year olds. She's a mentor.

Andres is absent. He won't come into the limelight. So I imagine him on top of a mountain looking the other way. Why is he so elusive? I ache to know.

One by one all my characters appear, teasing me to guess their full story.

Finally Jerome and Rachel arrive. They enter—smiling shyly—they don't want fame. A thousand tiny stars fall softly onto their heads. And now there's Abrahán. How does he fit in?

THE COLOURS IN THE SKY are still vivid. Above me is the other village shop surrounded by busy chickens, lazy dogs and ginger cats. I bought a bar of chocolate there, earlier. A dirty white hen strutted past my ankles, examining the shelves, pecking everything. She seemed to be taking an inventory.

With my bare feet enjoying the cool damp grass, I sit and watch the sun sink slowly until all the colours leave the sky. It is a spectacular show of coral reds, oranges and dusky blues: flaming Chinese warriors melt into sea horses; sea horses transform into gentle, leaping, wild grey goats. I'm unable to leave till the last bit of colour slides over the edge of the world and night-time embraces the tiny village I'm beginning to fall in love with.

I WANDER SLOWLY BACK to the cabin and find the table set with two places. There's a plate of cheese and crackers, chunks of home made bread, a slab of pâté and some sweet biscuits.

"Good timing," says Abrahán, pulling back a chair back for me to sit down.

"How was it?" he asks, pasting pâté onto a cracker.

"Wonderful," I say.

We eat in silence and I begin to experience another wave of intense emotions. They slide though my whole being, just like the sunset. But they don't disappear off the edge of the world. They somehow slip slowly into that bottomless heart space where memory, experience and hope live together. I allow myself to understand that I am being cared for. Looked after. Possibly treasured.

THE NEXT MORNING I open the kitchen door to a smell of burning.

"You didn't smell anything during the night?" Abrahán asks with a worried look. I see the kitchen door is open and one of the dogs is sniffing a jet black ball.

"My bread rolls," he says seriously. "I put them in the oven last night to rise and forgot them! The kitchen was thick with black smoke when I arrived at seven. You didn't smell anything?"

The dog abandons the black roll. Abrahán says he's making more bread. My bus leaves at ten o'clock, maybe half past nine; it depends on something or other, so I'm better to be there by a quarter past nine. There's just time for a quick cup of tea and a cracker. After I pay my bill, which is next to nothing, Abrahán offers me a small silver plate with three wrapped sweets on it. I accept the gift as if it's a diamond necklace. It feels like one. And as we say goodbye under the ancient eucalyptus tree he bends down and kisses me tenderly on both cheeks. *"Te quiero, Margarita,"* he says—"I love you".

THE BUS DOESN'T ARRIVE at nine thirty. Lorena, Abrahán's shy daughter-in-law, walks along the road and surprises me by sitting down on the bench beside me. We're facing the three-storied hostal with the shop below, where Sabine, Peter and I tried to stay that first night. It feels like a month ago now. Lorena asks me how old I think she is. I think she's very young, about twenty eight. She astonishes me by saying she's nearly fifty. Then she launches into a tragic story of how unhappy she is. How they couldn't continue with the boat business anymore.

"My heart is broken," she says.

"Does Abrahán know?" I ask.

"Yes," she says, "he does."

The bus arrives and about twelve people clamber off. It's a breakfast and toilet stop, but there's no café open, the hostal's closed, so people buy an assortment of things to satisfy their breakfast needs: chocolate, crisps, some have brought sandwiches wrapped in tin foil. They disperse around the village street. A man arrives and unlocks the village hall where the toilet is.

"You'll know when to leave," I say to Lorena. "When the time is right you'll just know in every bone of your body,

174

then it's easy because there's nothing else to be done. Until then, it's not time. Just time to think about what you really want for yourself." She disappears with a very sad smile and a thank you.

"Thank you for sharing your story with me," I say.

A STRETCH OF THE CARRETERA AUSTRAL FROM THE BUS

VILLAGE HOUSE

Chapter 20

WE STOP AT RIO TRANQUILO FOR LUNCH. Lenin's caravan is still parked opposite the one-pump petrol station/café. I think it's a permanent fixture. The sign for the boat trips to the marble caves is still up; the season hasn't quite finished. I look at the beach and long to see Jerome and Rachel dancing there, just one more time. I picture Ashley and Lindsey scuttling about, guidebook under arm, gathering transport information.

WE ARRIVE BACK at Coyhaique just before dark and this time I have a plan.

At the same bus station where I fist saw Jerome and Rachel clambering onto the bus with all their bags, I see a taxi and wave to the driver.

"Yes," he says, "but I have another passenger as well." An elderly lady pushes herself into his front seat and I hop into the back.

"The Spanish language school," I say. "You know it?"

"Of course I know it," comes the hoarse reply.

We speed off. Oh dear, it's turning out to be a long, long way from the centre of town. When the taxi finally stops I ask him to wait, explaining I haven't got a reservation at the school. In a park opposite, a brass band cranks up and plays a triumphal tune which I wonder might be a big sign from the universe that this is absolutely it!

No. This is absolutely not it.

Herr Gruff, the director, is gruffer then he was on the phone when I called him from Spain. The room he shows me is just as Alyssa described it. She only stayed here one night. It's waiting for a radical make-over. Herr Gruff is now speaking to me in English because he reckons my Spanish isn't up to much. He insists his wife will be home soon and "will do what's necessary for good stay here with lessons, yes. How you want lesson?"

"Umm …?"

"How you want lesson?" he raises his voice.

"Morning? Afternoon? All day?"

I take my leave saying I feel I'm too far away from town. Herr Gruff doesn't seem bothered at all. The taxi driver with the elderly lady is annoyed to have been kept waiting so long and the triumphal music has stopped.

"Where now?" he asks.

"Oh, just drop the lady off and I'll check the guidebook," I splutter.

We drive miles around the town and finally drop our senior citizen off in a seedy suburb.

"Where now?" asks the tired driver.

"The converted sawmill, please," I say.

"More, more," mimes my chauffeur rubbing his thumb against his fingers.

"Oh hey, of course," I say, "I know, it's another ride— fine—is it near?"

"Not really."

THE CONVERTED SAWMILL sounds fascinating in the guidebook, but when we arrive it's extremely posh. This is the most luxurious hotel I've seen in South America so far.

The taxi driver wheels Shamus into the foyer and I notice antique sofas, large glass bowls full of exotic flowers and a few rich-looking young businessmen deep in conversation. The owner arrives and tells me they have no vacancies. It's getting dark. I'm tired. It's Coyhaique again. I feel I'm possibly being denied a room because I look scruffy. I start to feel scruffy. Whether this is true or not, the proprietor takes it upon himself to ring another hotel for me. Full too. He tries another. Also full. The third, also full. I'm beginning to think I'll have to go back to Neena when he has a brainwave. Hotel Alicia. The answer is yes. So off we speed again.

"Another fare," the taxi driver reminds me.

When we get to the hotel, the taxi driver is halfway up the stairs with Shamus when the receptionist tells me a new price. I almost create a scene.

"Put the case down," I shout to the driver.

"Stop, stop, stop. Listen," I say. "You said twenty pesos on the phone five minutes ago. But now you are asking me for thirty."

"What do you want to pay?" the woman asks bluntly.

"Not more than twenty," I say.

She disappears into the kitchen and returns quickly.

"OK," she says. "Twenty! This is your room."

My room is right beside the front door. The taxi driver, who has finally become my ally, disappears, and I sink onto a single bed exhausted and switch on the TV. The news blares something about riots somewhere. I'm too tired to concentrate. I think Santiago is mentioned. Probably something to do with Pinochet in the recent past I think. Wrong. But, as always I get what I need and what I need is supper followed by a good sleep, not a massive scare. That will follow tomorrow.

SO FAR, HALF MY NEW PLAN HAS COLLAPSED. No Spanish lessons. I leave my room and go in search of supper. As before, gangs of not too fierce-looking dogs patrol the main streets looking for interesting rubbish to eat. They're looking for supper too. We're all hungry.

The restaurant near the plaza is bright, busy and welcoming and the vegetable soup is delicious. The German cakes on display look even more fabulous than the cakes we bought in Cochrane and when mine arrives, a three-tier creation filled with toffee cream, I say to the waitress:

"I couldn't possibly eat all of that. It's enough for three people!"

"Take it home, then," she says. "Eat a bit here and I'll wrap the rest up for you."

Superlatives cannot describe the next six mouthfuls, the next five minutes. Leaving the restaurant, I see the elderly tramp I saw last time, sitting on the pavement, his back leaning against the same lamppost. He looks like a cross between the old biblical gentleman at Tortel and Abrahán. His face is beautiful and he greets me.

"Hello, how are you?"

It's like he's known me all his life. He's surrounded by dirty plastic bags and sniffing dogs. His shoes are rags. My carryout cake feels like stolen goods in my hand. Will I give it to him? Of course I will. But my thoughts are travelling too slowly and I'm past him before I know what I feel I want to do. As a result, back in the warm hotel room I experience another set of emotions which lead me nowhere as they all conclude that my life is OK and his isn't, which I don't believe to be true. My last self-sabotaging thought accompanies the wasting of half of the leftover cake into the rubbish bin the next morning.

Black mark, Meg. Be more alert.

THE NEXT MORNING I decide to move camp. Wherever I decide to go from here, there is no bus north till tomorrow. I need to get new information about the ferry—it should leave in two days time. The prospect of a slow sail north on a local cargo ferry is intoxicating. But the first priority is to find somewhere cheaper to stay, somewhere where I can cook. Guidebook in hand, I trudge around Coyhaique for hours and find places far worse than Neena's, or they are closed for the season.

With a feeling of defeat I finally hail a taxi. Neena opens her kitchen door with a fleeting smile. She shows me the room next to the one I had last time and it's a notch better. I ask her for directions to the ferry info office and the bus depots. There are four. She's busy, not interested and gabbles the info quickly. Too quickly.

The ferry info draws a blank, again. I'm told there might be the chance of a ticket if I wait until the fifth, seven days from today, but maybe not. I'm thinking about Andres and secretly, impatiently, longing to see him again. Nobody's sure still if the ferry will run. Seven days in Coyhaique? No, I don't think so.

Then follows two hours of complete disorientation. I'm trying to find the bus depot. Neena's instructions begin to feel like a spell she's cast on me. I keep asking people for help and I keep literally going round in circles. I've been back to the wrong depot three times. I can't find the Don Carlos office anywhere. It's Don Carlos who goes north tomorrow; another bus company will leave in two days. Finally I find Don Carlos and—surprise surprise—it is the same bus depot we landed at when I first arrived at Coyhaique!

I buy my ticket and set off to find Javier again, the stone carver beside the plaza.

"I can't teach you anything in an afternoon," he says, rather scornfully, in response to my question. He shows me huge calluses on his nicotine-stained index fingers.

"Stone carving's very hard and takes a long time. There's a lot to learn, different kinds of stone, different tools."

I was just wondering if we could start this afternoon, *then* have a week's lessons, that's what I meant to say. I'm thinking I'll change my bus ticket. Wouldn't mind staying at Neena's for a week if I could learn this skill, just enough so that I could write on stones on the beach, draw angels on rocks in the mountains, things like that.

"No, no." Javier shakes his head seriously. "Not possible."

With a sinking feeling I realise I haven't made myself clear at all.

"Here's my website," says the tired stone carver, "and if you come back next year to stay, email me and we'll arrange something."

He's forgotten we've already met. Javier looks at me intently, possibly patronisingly. I think he's being kind, but I feel stupid and deflated because I've been misunderstood—another personality flaw. I buy a small stone on which he's beautifully drawn a mountain hare. He charges me half what he asked for it the last time. The weary man with so much talent shakes my hand and another dream fades.

THE NEW LARGE SUPERMARKET near Neena's home has only five cars in the car park. Outside, indigenous women sit on camp stools or stand in front of large blue cool boxes. They call their wares and open their boxes to hand out foil-wrapped *empanadas* or hot potato croquettes to hungry passers-by. I'm easily tempted. They watch me eat my steaming *empanada* sitting on a wall beside them. I'm the best joke of the day.

"Good!" they shriek.

"You like them? Yes?"

"Lovely," I reply.

"Want another one?"

"Ok, I'll try the other kind."

The dogs hover around hopefully. The next delicacy is the croquette with meat chunks. The potato is delicious but the meat is not. I'm reminded of Renaldo's goat bone. A crowd of teenagers arrives and the ladies are inundated with new customers. Lucky for me and lucky for the dogs.

BETWEEN LEAVING the supermarket and sitting in front of Neena's TV in the kitchen where the bad news arrives, I review my options now.

Option One is to wait seven days for the ferry which may or may not sail. This will take me north to Andres's town, Chaiten. Then, after a few days getting to know 'the beautiful legend', I'd arrive by eight-seater plane in Puerto Montt, followed by another flight to Santiago

Option Number Two has just crashed: no Spanish lessons and no stone-carving classes.

Option Number Three: go back by road to Casa Redonda. Bus back up the beautiful Carretera Astral though Puyuhuapi. After my 'mission days' with Andres, take the eight-seater plane to Puerto Montt, then the jet back to Santiago, arriving on Good Friday.

It's Easter next weekend, so whatever happens this week, I've booked a night in Santiago.

As I open the kitchen door and find Neena sitting at the table—expressionless,—I know for certain sure I'm not going to wait here seven days for the ferry. I'm going to leave by bus tomorrow and head for the Round House. The pull, the voice, the star, are all yelling. Moments after I have these thoughts, I get the fright of my life. Well, the fright of the trip.

Chapter 21

"TEA?" SUGGESTS NEENA, her dark brown, wavy hair covering half her face. I sit beside her and watch the drama unfold above us on the wall mounted TV. Santiago has become a war zone. Thousands of youths are storming the city, setting fire to everything that's flammable. Armies of riot police are charging. There's gunfire, panic and chaos. It's terrifying.

"Most of those kids are under fifteen," Neena informs me.

I peer to see if this could be true. It's the annual day to commemorate the killing of two boys gunned down in the Pinochet regime. Every year there's a rally which sometimes turns nasty. This year, apparently, the police were expecting trouble but not on this scale. It's truly horrific. Hundreds of the new buses have been burned to shells. There's footage of the bus depots with charred wreckage. How are people going to get to work now, I wonder?

I'm very alarmed, selfishly, as to how I'm going to get home to Spain, if this continues? But it doesn't. Later in the evening there's more footage about the damage and scenes of police stations in Santiago full of thirteen to sixteen year old boys with their parents. The boys are too young to be charged. Neena is philosophical about the news, though it's worse this year than usual, she says. It's impossible to imagine what she really feels.

A BRISK ENERGETIC HIKE INTO THE COUNTRYSIDE outside the town fills a few hours and gradually clears my fear. The terracotta coloured mountains and yellow ochre fields, the dry, burnt umber earth edging the silvery river stones, the grey water and the winding dusty dirt track roads, the sun burnt grasses and dogs playing noisily, all draw me into the now. I'm not in Santiago yet. According to Neena, the teenage 'war' may well be over in twenty four hours. She should know.

I'm just twelve hours away from Andres now. The legend glides into my thoughts like a beautiful condor overhead. Whatever happens in the capital city, I decide, I'm going to Chaiten. My intuition is on red alert in all directions. I'm certain sure this man holds the secret to some major part of the film story.

But, as I walk, I begin to wonder if I could be focusing on the wrong angle of the Andres legend? Am I looking through the binoculars back to front, so to speak? Could this pull be something to do with his daughters, those enchanting little three and four year olds? Is there a link here to my own story of loss? Is my film's theme hidden in here somewhere? What happens when people don't recover from the death or disappearance of their child? Is there anything sadder than losing a child through miscarriage, abortion, still-birth, abduction, disappearance or illness? Is the death of a child synonymous with the loss of bliss in some part of the soul? Is it possible to re-find true connectedness, real bliss again, or does one have to live half a life thereafter, paying the price of karma, or guilt, or a thousand what-ifs? Will I give Rachel this challenge? Will I work out for her what I need to learn myself?

THE NEXT MORNING at seven, a taxi arrives to take me to the bus depot. Neena has left me a breakfast picnic on the kitchen table: a saucer of new, sticky, red rosehip jam, some flat round yeast-free bread and a packet of decaf coffee. The ancient, black woodstove with the two ovens is still burning. The row of cushions on the bench behind still has Neena's husband's shape indented on them.

OUTSIDE THE PADLOCKED BUS DEPOT GATES waits a young couple, their bikes resting against a wall. Clare, a wilderness sports instructor, and Ian, a vet from Australia, are cycling the whole thousand kilometres of the Carretera Austral. At this point they've decided to cheat. The road so far has been way beyond their expectations. After days of having their teeth and bones rattled incessantly, mending numerous punctures and other minor bike problems, plus braving a few storms, they've decided to have a holiday from their marathon, and take the famous Don Carlos bus north for the next four hundred kilometres. They're heading for Chaiten and the ferry north.

Then another young couple arrive, weighed down with large backpacks, eating sandwiches, carrying water bottles. Andy is a twenty-something, tattooed bookie from London with earrings; Angela, his partner, is a lawyer from Sheffield. They've both taken a year out from their jobs to explore the world, though Ladbrokes are keeping in touch with Andy because he seems to be indispensable to their new website. They've just done Asia and Australia!

Our driver arrives and instructs Ian to dismantle both bikes. He then begins the complicated task of filling the back of the small bus with piles of boxes, bike parts, cases and other cargo.

"Put the bike frames inside the bus," the driver shouts. "No—not there—in between the seats, in the aisle, *coño!*"— "Dickhead!"

It will be a twelve hour journey to Chaiten. I'm planning to get off at the halfway point, which is Puyuhuapi. I ask the driver if he's sure there will be another bus tomorrow.

"Maybe," he replies. "The other bus is being repaired right now."

"How likely is it it'll be fixed by tomorrow?"

"It's possible."

"But not probable?"

"Yes possible, but not probable," he replies with a laugh. He laughs, I laugh.

"If not tomorrow," he grins, "the next bus will be in three days, most likely."

I don't know why, but I'm certain sure possible is going to be probable.

THE SCENERY WE PASS on this return journey takes me into a state of pure awe. This love I have for Chile feels unquenchable. The landscape is so untouched, so unspoilt by man. Its silence and vastness are immense.

By contrast, as the bus hurtles on, Ian fills the space between us with masses of questions about my life in Spain. He munches a packet of biscuits which he is happy to share. I decline. I can't seem to stop his flow of questions. I don't want to be unfriendly, but I don't want to miss a minute of these spectacular views, and I want to remember everything I know so far about Andres, and his beautiful little daughters. Why is Ian not looking out of the window?

Finally, he tells me he's thinking of living in Spain for a year. I feel used, annoyed, irritated and cross with myself for feeling these feelings. Then I pretend to fall asleep, briefly and clean the inner slate.

We arrive at Puyuhuapi at about one o'clock. Andy and Angela decide to break the journey here too. I've told both couples about the enchanting Round House and their interest is fired. I say nothing about the charismatic Andres, they'll soon find out for themselves. Clare nips into the bus shack/office and calls Gabor. As the bus leaves in a cloud of dust, the beautiful wilderness sports instructress, whose father taught her to meditate for an eighteenth birthday present, and the handsome young restless vet, wave through a dirty window. I've warned them about Gabor's mood swings.

IT'S LOVELY TO BE BACK in beautiful Puyuhuapi with all my recent memories of it. I see Jo, the thin boat builder, in his garden and Lena, daughter of the famous pioneer, striding though the village in gumboots, deep in thought. Vera's teddy bear cabins are a stone's throw from the bus stop, but I decide to check out the hostal where I had lunch in the family's dining room by mistake. The rooms are clean and bright and the dining room upstairs has a picture postcard view down the fjord. Andy and Angela take the other room.

In the evening, I decide to visit the smallest restaurant in the world, the wooden shed which sits in the middle of a lush vegetable patch at the edge of the fjord. Andy and Angela decide to eat leftovers from their lunch. Inside the cafe I find two tables; one is occupied by three road workers. A sizzling sound comes from behind the kitchen door.

"Knock," says one of the men jerking his head towards the smell of hot oil. Ana offers me meat and chips, or *merluza*—hake—and chips. The men continue talking and drinking local wine. Their conversation changes tempo when I sit down. They're not sure how much Spanish I speak or understand. When their food arrives their plates are stacked high and steaming.

Their banter changes to a trickle. They laugh and grunt and loosen their belts. I hope she isn't going to give me so much.

My fish arrives with fresh vegetables from the garden. It's extremely tasty. The men swagger out, and I watch the sun set slowly over the narrow ultramarine fjord. It's wonderful, this feeling of being at home in South America.

THE NEXT MORNING I'M PACKED AND READY for the one o'clock bus. There's plenty of time to explore the carpet factory again. I head for the shed I missed last time and find four middle-aged women sitting on stools hard at work. The shed is large and dark; five of the six looms lie empty. A radio on a shelf in the corner broadcasts a programme on breast cancer. Beside it sits a jar of Nescafé and four orange mugs. The women ignore me, working and listening silently to their thoughts, or to the radio, or both. They're six hours away from the nearest hospital here.

It's a sombre atmosphere. I take some photos unobtrusively, as the light is fabulous, casting shadows on the women's darting hands. The shuttles make harsh, repetitive, rhythmic noises, punctuated by dry coughs and the occasional soft shuffling of feet. By chance, all the women are wearing something red. With brown, weather-beaten faces, they concentrate intently on the intricate pattern they're weaving. This is an intense team task; everybody knows exactly what's required of her and when—or if—one slows everybody patiently waits.

This is the legacy of Lena's father and the three other intrepid pioneers. Their dream is still very much alive and flourishing.

Then out in the bright fresh air again, magnetically I get drawn by the sound of the church bell. I have a strong suspicion I'm edging towards the unexpected, for better or worse. It's a strange kind of day. It's also Palm Sunday. Inside the dark blue wooden church, two local women and a seven year old boy busily ignore my entrance. I sit down about six rows from the front. Without any preamble the mass starts. I feel strangely invisible. The brown ceiling, the cream-coloured walls and the well-trodden wooden floor are all remains of yet another part of the pioneers' dream. I briefly imagine a wedding taking place here, a funeral, a baptism. The older of the two women reads from a folded leaflet.

Why is it that when certain unexpected things press certain hidden buttons, out tumbles a wretched rag-doll of a person, an ancient useless persona, a deflated, meaningless, valueless caricature of myself?

It was the palms that did it.

Or rather the substitute palms. Branches of an unidentifiable local tree. There's a little pile of them sitting on the floor in front of the altar. The two women and the little boy brandish theirs. I'm not offered one. I notice they're using the same printed sheets as we had at Tortel. This tells me there is no local priest, villagers guide themselves through mass.

One of the women is European-looking, middle-aged and confident. The other is part-indigenous. The little boy is bored and roams the pews dusting them with his branch. There's a brisk tone to the mass.

A dishevelled, pale-faced, youngish fisherman enters the church and sits near the front. The child immediately rushes to the altar, picks up a branch and with a shy smile which the man ignores, thrusts the fake palm into his arms.

"Papa," he says. "Papa."

The mass continues. The child cuddles into his dad like an affectionate puppy. The man takes no notice whatsoever. Father and son examine their branches. I leave the church feeling all the old dreadful feelings of being the outsider— not welcome, a fish out of water, unacceptable and odd and the biggie—the fatherless orphan! I send out a desperate dart of a prayer. It's a long time since this has happened God, so please help me. Quickly.

IT'S NEARLY HALF PAST TWELVE so I'm ready for the one o'clock bus, sitting outside Juan's shack, picnic lunch gobbled in case the bus comes early. By one thirty the bus hasn't appeared. At two o'clock Juan arrives to tell me the (repaired) bus hasn't left Coyhaique. There were no passengers waiting, so it didn't leave.

"But there are three of us waiting here," I say. Well, actually there aren't. Where are Andy and Angela?

Juan's eyebrows rise and fall. I remember my conversation with the driver at the bus depot yesterday:

"How likely is it the bus will leave tomorrow for Chaiten?"

"It's possible, but not probable."

How silly of me to think probable could be possible. The next bus will pass in three days time.

I'm determined to leave today. Andres is now only about eight hours away. But now it doesn't seem possible. No, I'm not going to hitchhike. Not with Shamus. I'm stumped, disappointed, ridiculously upset and still deeply bruised after the church fiasco. And I've forgotten to go with the flow. Some angry words with God follow. I explain to Him/Her/It that I need special help when I become this rag-doll person. I don't think I can wait much longer. Please help right now. Help arrives about half an hour later.

Chapter 22

I WANDER SLOWLY BACK to the hostal and ask for my room for another night.

"No problem," says the owner kindly.

Suddenly Andres and my quest to find his story feel blocked. I'm wildly disappointed. The escalating, overwhelming longing to know this man is irrational, intense and unquenchable. Right now I don't think my theme has anything to do with his daughters. It's him. Somehow my heart has been hooked by an invisible thread and I can't get free. I feel I'm being reeled in, drawn ashore.

I don't unpack Shamus, but decide to meander along the shore, maybe a coffee and a piece of delicious chocolate cake at Vera's café will do the trick, lift the grey cloud of disappointment.

Strolling towards the beach, I see four new silver Land Rover Discovery four- by-fours parked outside the café. A stylish logo *Vuelto al Mundo* is printed in black on each bonnet. A couple of extremely attractive young women, looking like models for an expensive sportswear brochure, stroll back towards the café, swinging digital cameras—smiling, laughing. I'm intrigued. What's going on?

VERA IS TAKING ORDERS for coffee and cakes from a group of about twelve beautiful people. She greets me like an old friend and I ask for a coffee. Finding an empty seat in the far corner, I'm just beginning to check this group out when somebody asks me where I'm from.

"Spain," I say.

"Oh!" They all swivel round in their chairs and beam.

"We are too. Where do you live?"

"Las Alpujarras."

"Really? How amazing! We're from Madrid."

All of them know my area. They've either been there recently, or have a relative there, or have spent their honeymoon there, or have been walking there. They all love Las Alpujarras. These wonderful, exuberant Spaniards start a process of adopting me and after a few more questions their fine-looking fifty year old leader— surely a famous film star?—decides I'm a kind of female Gerald Brennan.

"Where are you going next?" they ask. I tell them the story about the bus that didn't appear and won't appear for the next three days.

"Come with us," they say.

"We're going to Chaiten. We're leaving when we finish our coffee."

"Really?"

"Yes," they say. "There's plenty of room. Come. Are you packed?"

"Oh yes, I'm packed and ready!"

"Well let's roll then," says the leader and off I run to collect Shamus and the small orange backpack.

The jeeps sweep across the village in convoy and stop in front of my hostal. I'm to travel with Paco and Tina in the last jeep. Andy and Angela have gone to the alternative hot springs with Juan apparently. Being a lawyer, Angela needed concrete proof the bus would leave at one o'clock. I leave them a note.

There's space for sixteen people in the convoy. The two beautiful young women I saw swinging their cameras are Israeli hitchhikers. They've also been picked up today. Some of the other passengers are mechanics; a few are paying travellers. *Vuelto al Mundo* is an international, round-the-world race in four-by-fours. I'm now linked up with the Spanish team for their next leg. The team left Spain and drove right down through Africa, where they put the jeeps on a boat and sailed to the top of South America. Then they drove down through Brazil to Argentina and Tierra del Fuego. Now they're returning up the other side of South America, and are in a hurry.

We glide over the rough road effortlessly. No sick bags needed in this vehicle. Paco and Tina are a couple, not married they say, but a couple.

AFTER AN HOUR OUR CONVOY HALTS. The three silver four-by-fours in front have been creating a cloud of golden-brown dust behind them. Our adventure unfurls through a shimmering mysterious filter. It's like watching a film begin.

When we stop, our leader and the others are making their way, cameras in hand, to a roadside cattle sale. It's a hive of activity. The cowboys ride and herd the cattle with wild panache. The air is full of noise. Snorting calves, shouting men, whinnying horses. Dogs bark. Whips crack. People laugh. I don't hear a single mobile phone. There's a labyrinth of wooden walkways above the cattle pens, ingeniously built so that buyers look down onto the animals. Almost everything is happening underneath us. The young animals, in groups of about six, are herded in and out of pens, then onto a weighing grid. Next they're rushed into a small stadium.

Everything happens so fast. The cowboys, with their thick sheepskin trousers and back berets, turn their horses in unbelievably small spaces. Prospective buyers make decisions. Our group take a million photos. My camera refuses to work. It tells me *its memory is full*. It can't take any more beauty, or drama. I'm amused by the metaphor. But it's all a little scary, because if the walkway collapses, we're all going to be trampled to smithereens in seconds. The atmosphere is wild. The Israeli girls are photographing everything that moves, causing almost as much excitement as the animals themselves. Finally our leader says "¡*Vamos!*" and we pile back into the convoy and depart in another cloud of sepia dust.

"How long have you lived in Spain?" Tina asks me, as we speed beside an opal coloured river.

"Twelve years," I reply. "But during my first five years I 'migrated' to Alaska every May, then retuned to Andalucía in September. Parts of Patagonia remind me of Alaska. Have you been to Alaska?"

"Not yet."

"You speak Spanish very well," Paco interjects.

"Really? I don't think I do, but thanks for the encouragement. In the village where I live, the accent is very hard to understand. They break all the grammar rules and they drop the ends of lots of words!"

"We have trouble understanding the Andaluz accent too!" they both laugh.

"How many people live in your village?"

"About 68."

"Do you have a shop?"

"Yes—a very small one—and a bar."

"Are they still working the land?" Paco seems genuinely interested.

"A few still are. There were at least twenty working mules and donkeys in the village when I first arrived. Now there are only about seven."

We drive past more gigantic rhubarb plants lining both sides of the dirt track highway. So far we haven't passed another car.

"How far away is your nearest doctor?" asks Tina.

"The doctor actually comes to the village three times a week, with a nurse. A male nurse. Then he takes a surgery in a bigger village twenty minutes away. It's a clever system, because he takes all the prescriptions to the other village which has the pharmacy and a bakery and the next morning—very early—the baker brings the bread and the pills to our village. He leaves the pills in the house beside the church, so during the day people arrive to collect their medicines whenever they like."

Gentle guitar music fills the air-conditioned jeep. The quality of the sound is extraordinary, far better than anything I've ever heard before. But then, I just have an old walkman for travelling; an ancient radio-cassette player at home.

My thoughts slide back to images of the strong mules and the sturdy little donkeys ploughing the land in my magical village. I read somewhere that Herman Hesse the inspirational German author, tried to live his life as an unfolding fairly tale. I believe he felt he failed.

In many ways I'm living out the love of the peasant life I discovered in literature, all those years ago. I loved it in Russian, Eastern European and Chinese stories and particularly in the novels of Jewish Isaac Beshevis Singer.

The main difference now is that I don't need my village life—inner or outer—to be coloured or tainted by drama or tragedy. My years of addiction to sadness have melted into compassion and I think I've overcome my personal hunger for drama. So, life in the village feels like a gentle, unfolding poem and often like a beautiful, slow-moving, poetic fairytale. Every time I leave my house, I have an adventure with animals, neighbours or weather, or all three.

"How high are you in the mountains?" Paco interrupts my train of thought.

"About seven hundred metres," I say. "Not that high."

I show Tina a photo of my village. She passes it to Paco, who's driving.

"Do they still have *matanzas*?" Paco wants to know.

"Yes."

Tina turns right round to gauge my expression.

"They start in December I think. But there are fewer every year."

Matanzas are pig-killing rituals. My neighbours' lives are bound around the ancient rituals of each season. They work seven days a week. My taxi-ing them to and from our local market, to funerals or hospitals, is always thanked by bags of produce—figs, almonds, peaches, oranges, beans, wild herbs, flowers—whatever is being gathered, I'm given. And I don't have to taxi anybody anywhere for these gifts to arrive on my kitchen table.

"There's so much kindness and generosity in the village," I tell Tina and Paco. "I'm overwhelmed sometimes by how kind they are to me."

"The *campesinos* are very friendly in the south," Paco replies. "We'll come and visit you one day. We'll need a retreat after this race is over!"

"You'll be very welcome," I say, meaning it. Then I tell them about some of the village characters, starting with two of my favourites.

I PAINT A WORD PICTURE of elderly Angustia and the sainted Lola. Stocky, white-haired Lola—who only wears black—has terrible stomach problems. Dark wavy-haired, ample Angustia—always seen wearing one of her home made aprons—has bad legs. They're only ten years older than me but their skin is deeply wrinkled by years of outdoor living. Decades of sweltering summers have taken their toll. Their bodies are bent from planting and picking vegetables, milking goats, making cheese, collecting eggs, killing rabbits and chickens, drying figs, making sausages and rearing children. I adore these heroines with a passion.

I've decided both have been my mother in previous lives. Angustia, my nearest neighbour—now sadly afflicted with Alzheimer's and not living in the village any more—used to massage my back when it hurt. Her hands were the hands of an angel. I miss her more than words can say.

"One summer," I tell Tina, "Angustia taught me how to make soap. This ritual happens every three years. She makes it in her green, forty year old, plastic baby bath."

In the cool summer evenings, Angustia would spend hours telling me stories about her life as a young woman, living in another tiny village nearby, without electricity, without running water, no bathroom, no transport. It would be seven hours walk to visit the doctor in those days and nine—uphill—to return. She'd walk the twenty two kilometres carrying a sick child. Her life revolved around tending her animals, planting and harvesting crops and feeding her four children while her young husband searched for work in France. At night she'd find time to embroider. She loved to make and embroider aprons. Times have always been tough for country people in this part of Spain and Angustia's humble, hard-working husband, Miguel, picked fruit in France for years. Under his overalls he'd be wearing the white longjohns she'd lovingly made for him, embroidered with his initials in cobalt blue silk. Now and then I'd offer her Reiki healing for her seventy two year old sore legs.

"Yes please," she'd say. Then the next day she'd say, "I slept so well Margarita and the pain's gone. What did you do?" And when she saw my house—which had belonged to her sister—rebuilt and finished, she put her hands to her face and said:

"¡Madre mia de mi vida! How do you have room in your head for all these ideas?"

While Angustia was ploughing her fields with her mule, I was painting in my Kindergarten Heaven.

Lola—who only wears black nowadays—kisses me six times on each cheek when we meet. She greets me like I'm some fairy princess who's been lost in the forest for years. She's deaf in one ear and blind in one eye. Like Angustia, she doesn't speak, she shouts. Whenever I come across her on the mountain track in the late afternoon—sitting on a ridge beside her old husband, looking out into infinity, waiting for hours for her son-in-law to pick them up and drive them down to the village—I offer a lift. Sometimes she accepts, and if she does, she thanks me the next day with bags of onions and eggs or tomatoes and red peppers. Lola lost her son in a car accident. Unspoken, our old grief finds its counterpart when we meet and—like two clouds merging without effort—it dissolves into new love. We are intimately at home with each other, even though I only understand one word in twenty that she says.

I TELL TINA how I love being a part of village life. How I feel I've found where I belong in the world. I'm the quiet, exiled, Irish artist with the multi-coloured car who lives on her own and who built her own house.

In the early days when my Spanish is embarrassingly poor, I try to share my exile story with the gentle, lovely Loli—who has the magical garden—an angelic, forty year old mom with a heart of pure gold. What came out in terrible mangled Spanish must have sounded something like this:

"Irlundia—buorn Irlanda—adupted—beeig trouble—I go night boat."

I don't know how to say 'go back' so I continue:

"I no can go my country es mucho complicado. Leaf mi mama muy triste. Muy bad storiii." A few years later when my Spanish has improved, I'm able to share the real story with Loli. Our friendship is sealed for life.

"You actually built your own house?" asks Paco.

"Well—no—I didn't physically build my own house."

I laugh at the very thought.

"I designed it. I wanted it be full of visual surprises. And it is!"

I'd had a dream for the last six years that one day, when I finished being a nomad, I would buy a house and create an inspiring space for artists and writers to come and rest and re-charge. I'd also had a dream that this calm space would be used for recovery holidays, for people searching for creative support after bereavements, after a miscarriage, after divorces, after separations, after the loss of a job, or the loss of faith, or the loss of country and culture—exiles. People estranged from their inner voice.

And that dream came true. Over the last six years— thanks to the internet—people have come from all around the world to the village to make different kinds of retreats. The villagers extend their kindness to my guests and the beauty of the landscape works its magic.

"Two neighbours rebuilt the house for me," I continue. "It took a year and it took as long for the villagers to accept me."

Tina nods and smiles. I'm speaking to her profile.

"My neighbours love my paintings," I tell them. "Isn't that amazing? They really love them. Everybody in the village has been in my house at some time or another."

I PAINT ANOTHER WORD picture of the birthday parties I've given for my special women friends in the village— including the lovely, spiritual Loli with the long auburn hair, who left school aged fourteen, who always wears red, whose house is full of esoteric books, crystals and finely crocheted, red tablecloths. In this part of Spain adults don't seem to have the birthday party tradition we have in Scotland. They celebrate their saint's day instead. So I bake a cake and decorate it with candles, usually between thirty five and forty five. The entire village school arrives—all five of them— and with their mothers, they pile into my kitchen. We play silly games, like stick the tail on the donkey. They giggle and cheat; cheat and giggle. The kids have juice and the moms drink pints of village wine, eat tasty tapas and enjoy sticky chocolate cake. I buy a cheeky present, a skimpy G-string or a little bra with large tassels and the less shy neighbours try it on—over their clothes—and we'll laugh a lot.

"Gerardo was right," says Paco. "You sound like a modern day Gerald Brennen."

"No, not really," I say, laughing. "For a start I'm Irish, not English!"

Chapter 23

WE DRIVE THOUGH MORE extraordinary landscapes and I feel I'm travelling through yet another enchanted land. We even have the perfect music to fit this South American movie which is unfolding slowly in my head. But it's a film set without actors.

My interesting characters aren't here yet.

There're elsewhere.

Doing other jobs.

I can't get them to meet each other.

I can't hook any of them together.

There's the young busker with the unforgettable voice in the dingy tunnel. She's still in the tunnel.

There's the handsome, bare foot, winking pleasure-boat captain and the coquettish, whispering Babette and the sinking boat-load of rich tourists. The captain's still on his boat and Babette's still drinking wine on the lavender farm.

There's Neena—the witch who makes rosehip jam—and Javier the serious stone carver who smokes too much. They haven't moved from Coyhaique and they're not interested in each other.

The farmer with the kitten who's desperate for a foreign wife hasn't found her yet.

Renaldo's still doing his penance on crutches.

And Jerome and Rachel? Andres and Abrahán? There's no story line yet; no thread's coming.

Maybe—just maybe—I could transport some of my Spanish neighbours to Patagonia?

A new vision suddenly makes my whole being light up with a jolt. How amazing if all my characters were in the three jeeps in front of us! How incredible if this was the real thing. It's happened. The film's been written; the characters auditioned; we're on location. It's a French-Bolivian co-production—small budget—an art film which will take Cannes by storm in the year 2011.

Somehow it doesn't matter I haven't got the connections yet. There's no hurry. I know it'll unfold. How? The Voice again? There's magic at play here and just a few minutes after I think that thought, the alchemy starts again.

Tina changes the tape.

The new music is exotic, mystical, eastern, hypnotic.

"What's this called?" I ask. "Can I read the cover?"

Tina passes it over.

Sublime sounds fill the space between the three of us.

"Portals of Grace," she says. "Lovely isn't it?"

Portals of Grace lifts me into that other dimension. I'm gone. I'm no longer in my physical body. I'm on my way to join my characters for our first real meeting.

I read the CD notes. Azam Ali, the singer, the mezzo-soprano *"whose unforgettable voice has graced many major film scores"*, is Iranian. Her music combines medieval Sephardic Breton and Latin sources with ancient, Persian classical music. In a matter of moments Azam has taken me to the Source.

I'm wandering around out there in the ether, wanting to give Rachel a loving mother for my story. Will it be the resourceful and kind Angustia, or the adoring and simple Lola?

Then, like an inner tsunami, my imagination spirals off, and won't stop.

I SEE SEVENTEEN YEAR OLD aspiring singer/artist Rachel in her château home in southern France, surrounded by fields of purple lavender. She's leaning out of a window, watching her parents. She's crying.

In the driveway her forty five year old father paces around on the gravel. His elderly Bolivian driver/butler is standing beside an expensive car; he's looking up at Rachel, signalling something with a hand gesture. Rachel's mother Annabel is standing—wobbling—close to Aphrodite, a granite fountain/ statue surrounded by water lilies. A recurring family scene unfolds. I'm viewing it from the lawn. I witness Rachel's cruel, aristocratic, art-collector father Marcel—frequently away for months on business trips—shouting at her mother. He's telling her to stop drinking and leave.

"And take that idiot singer with you," he shouts, meaning Rachel. "And don't expect a penny from me." Pupils dilated, he's wild with rage. He's never believed Rachel is his daughter. The dates never fitted. Rachel's mother is lost to alcohol, so—so neither Angustia nor Lola can possibly be her mother.

Oh!

Now that's a surprise. The chateau scene fades. I'm in a hazy void. Azam Ali continues to sing.

I'm determined to give Rachel a loving character somewhere in her childhood, to teach her that love is a beautiful energy; that real love is never afraid. That unconditional love doesn't need alcohol to thrive. Could it be a man?

A grandfather? Her father's father? A Jew of Sephardic origin? A Rabbi? No—he's long since dead.

An Uncle? Her mother's brother? An American missionary in South America? No.

A brother? A twin? No. An older brother? No. Her older brother dies aged four of leukaemia. Marcel never gets over this. Annabel takes to the bottle.

A local priest? No. Annabel and Marcel have given up on God.

A family retainer? Yes? Yes—it's Joel. The wise Bolivian gardener/valet who plants vegetables by the moon's cycles, whose free time and loving care is given unconditionally to baby Rachel, to young Rachel, then to adult Rachel. He teaches her all he knows about planting, waiting, watching and harvesting. He teaches her that everything in life—the joys and the sorrows, the challenges and the successes—all have a season. Yes. It's Joel—the unusual, chauffeur/butler/spiritual odd-job man/gardener. He's her teacher.

What's his back story?

He's adored Rachel since the moment she slithered from her mother's pickled womb with surprisingly tanned skin and thick, dark hair. With her father away on frequent business trips, it is Joel who frequently looks after baby Rachel in the nursery, whilst her mother lies unconscious in the master bedroom after days of binge drinking.

So how does he come to live in the château?

Orphaned Joel—the indigenous, charming, colourful Bolivian, a waiter, aged twenty four, accompanied by his beautiful, young, pregnant, dancer wife Susanna—arrives in Marseille on a cargo boat from South America. Susanna soon becomes incurably homesick and falls in love with a Chilean sailor. A year later, word reaches Joel that Susanna is living in Santiago. She's given birth to his daughter. Brokenhearted, gentle Joel vows never to marry again. For years he drifts from job to job, waiter, gardener, odd-job man, butler; never managing to save enough money for his fare home.

Aged forty five and in his prime, he's employed as a driver/valet/gardener/odd-job-man by rich, French aristocrat Marcel, who lives in a luxurious chateau in the south of France with his coquettish and beautiful young American wife, Annabel. Surprisingly, Joel becomes religious a year after the birth of Rachel.

THE MUSIC and the air conditioning in the jeep keep me suspended in my altered state. I'm hovering in a different dimension, not noticing or hearing or feeling anything except these inner images.

I SEE THE KIND AND HANDSOME Joel—now sixty— standing beside Marcel's Bentley. It's parked to the side of the seventeenth century château. Behind him, in the landscaped grounds with the pine forest to the east, I see some of Rachel's art installations: there's a domed shelter made from grey-green willow branches, adorned with white jasmine scattered on the roof and the floor; it's her shelter for dreaming. To the left, she's threaded hundreds of scarlet berries on invisible catgut and strung them—like a string of beads—between two giant pine trees. Small birds, dragonflies and colourful butterflies bounce and rest on them. Around the roots of four mighty pines, she rearranged their fallen fir cones, making exquisite patterns, circles radiating outwards in different shades of browns. Another line of threaded berries—these ones poisonous and snowy white—floats like a thousand pearls on the surface the deep brown fish pond.

"If something lasts only briefly, like my installations, can it still be full of meaning?" asks Rachel.

"Is it possible to do no harm in the world, to make every touch matter?"

Joel, the butler/gardener has been Rachel's devoted friend since the day of her birth, is the person who attempts to answer all her metaphysical questions.

Time fast forwards. The scenario moves on.

It's the same scene a year later, a château in the sunny south of France. Rachel, eighteen, is now on the gravel with her mother. Her mother's still wobbling beside the fountain. Joel stands beside the car looking worried. A suitcase and a backpack are brought and dumped by Annabel's maid/ companion Hildegard, the bad-natured German who loathes men. Marcel is shouting the same message he shouts regularly. A motor bike arrives, drowning his voice. A young man dressed in leather, pierced with rings and studs, whose whole neck is tattooed with snakes, shouts to Rachel.

"Ready?"

Rachel picks up her backpack and awkwardly heaves herself onto the back of the motor bike, her bulging belly obviously heavily pregnant. They disappear northwards. Marcel screams at Annabel to get into the car and never, ever come back. Hildegard appears with another case and the two women are driven to the train station by a distressed Joel, who buys them single tickets for Paris.

Although his liaison with Annabel only lasted a drunken half-hour eighteen years ago—a secret which will accompany him to his grave—Joel's heart is in tatters. The thought of Rachel living in squalor in bohemian Montmatre, with his grandchild, and Annabel, left to an unknown fate, also in Paris with the miserable Hildegard, slowly turns him into a new man, a thief.

Every month he sends most of his wages to Rachel. The child is born; it's a daughter. Rachel's partner, a heroine addict, leaves her. Joel steals an icon painting from the château and arrives in Paris to explain his plan to Rachel. He'll sell the painting and they'll emigrate to Bolivia. He has many friends in La Paz who will look after them, he promises. Annabel will reach rock bottom before finding a Mexican shaman who changes her life for ever.

So, Jerome, can I give *him* a lovely mother? Will it be Angustia or Lola?

OUR JEEP CONTINUES ITS RACE to Chaiten, following fast flowing turquoise rivers and ancient pristine forests. Outside, night time is silently falling all around us but I see and hear nothing except my inner journey. I'm lost in my inner tsunami. Now it sweeps me off to Bolivia.

JEROME. I HEAR HIM SCREAMING his way into a cruel world. His mother's a young Bolivian wrestler learning her trade. On the way home after a fight she's lost, dazed and weakened, she's attacked by a white man twice her weight and left raped in the gutter. Nine months later she gives birth to a boy alone, in a hovel of an old seamstress's shop, where she works by day. She wraps the child in scraps of coloured cloth, enclosing a photo of herself as a young girl and all the money she possesses in the world—which amounts to 225 Bolivian Bolivianos—about twenty euros. Bullied by her elderly, ill father who persuades her that the child will be born cursed for life and will bring curses on the family, she dumps the baby bundle beside a rubbish bin and returns to her retired, wrestler-mother's back room to cry and bleed.

Claudio, a twelve year old country boy, passes the rubbish bin and finds the child. He's been sent by Lola, his mother, to find work in the city; his father's been killed in a political rally.

Lola, desperately torn between sending her beloved son to the dangerous city or watching her three other small children die of hunger, lives in a village seven hours walk from La Paz. The innocent bread-winner, Claudio, picks up the baby and discovers the hidden money, enough to feed his family for at least three months. With the newborn in his arms Claudio begins to run the long distance home. After two hours he's stopped by an American in a car. The stranger demands to know what the boy is up to. Terrified Claudio refuses to talk. A storm breaks out. Rain lashes down. The American persuades Claudio to allow him to drive him to his village. During the drive, Claudio tells him the story. The foreigner is an aid worker. A new, European-funded, community project is about to begin locally; the American promises he'll get in touch.

Claudio arrives at his mother's house with the brand new baby, the money and the photo. Lola, deaf in one ear and blind in one eye, shouts in horror. Not another mouth to feed? She doesn't understand the baby's arrived with rent money. Patiently Claudio manages to explain. Lola begins to lavish all her love on the baby boy who grows up to be strong, kind and loving, just like his replacement mother. When the infant's three months old—they've called him Jerome—the money runs out. Once again Lola tells Claudio he'll have to go to the city to find work. As he prepares to leave, the American turns up and Claudio gets a job with a new water plant that's about to be installed in the village.

Ten years later, the family are well and Jerome is a joy to everybody. He's a little clown by nature and a hard worker.

Lola has bought a locket and put the photo he arrived with in it. Jerome wears the locket night and day. They think the girl in the photo must be his sister.

The political situation is worsening and every week men, women and children go missing, or are killed. Tragedy strikes one day when, without any warning, Lola, Claudio and the three younger children are hauled out of their adobe house into the street and shot. The soldiers torch the house. Jerome is in the tiny pig shed behind the house, feeding the animals, when this happens. His world falls apart. He becomes a street-kid and takes to drugs.

Within a year he's locked up in an institution for boys who've committed serious crimes. Every week a man called Ivan comes to the prison to teach the boys circus skills. Two years later, Ivan adopts seven of the boys, including Jerome, whose sentences have finished. He takes them to his home, cares for them and teaches them how to teach other street-children circus skills. Within a short time the little troop have formed a street theatre. They express all their desperate feelings though drama and circus arts and the children gradually find a sense of self-worth and a purpose in life. After a few years, their theatre project becomes a huge and growing success and Ivan is invited—and funded—to take part in street festivals in Europe, with the children. This becomes an annual event. When Jerome is twenty one, he travels to Paris with Ivan. This is where he meets Rachel, in Montmatre. Rachel is in serious trouble.

TWO HOURS LATER OUR CONVOY stops again, this time to photograph a wooden church on stilts. Beside it a cowboy is wrestling with a bull. The bull has a rope tied around its head and the cowboy's on horseback. The bull doesn't want to be pulled into the field. A battle of wills is being played out. The Israeli girls head for the church. I notice a clump of trees on the other side of the road and disappear.

When I emerge I find Tina talking to our leader. I know immediately they're talking about me and wonder what to do. I'm still not quite back from my inner journeying.

"I'm telling him all about you," smiles Tina. This man is so handsome he's dazzling.

"What does it say?" he asks me, staring at my chest.

I look down on the machine-embroidered, upside-down, blue J on my old blue fleece.

"Just J," I say.

"No," he says coming closer. I stand still. Some squiggly lines running though the J spell *joie de vivre.*

"Oh," I say. "I honestly never noticed."

"How appropriate," he says with a beautiful smile. And with these human words and that smile, my spell is broken and Jerome's story vanishes for the next four months. I forget it.

BACK IN CONVOY AGAIN, it's getting towards dusk. A full moon will soon be with us. Tina—camcorder in hand— speaks into the mike describing the landscape as we drive. Her Spanish words sound exquisite. It doesn't seem possible that the setting can get any more beautiful than this, but it does, it's beyond words, even Spanish words and when the full moon slides up above the snow peaks, I feel ecstatic. Everything is happening here: music, friendship, meeting my characters, fabulous nature, full moon. Eight hours ago I was a wretched rag-doll. Now I'm experiencing Portals of Grace. Thank you God. Palm Sunday not to be forgotten.

We glide into Chaiten. Tina has booked the group into a comfortable hotel in advance. The team plan to catch the ferry to the mystical island of Chiloé tomorrow morning. I tell them the ferry leaves late tonight, about half past eleven. They didn't know. By chance, we find we've stopped right outside their hotel. Everybody piles out. The beautiful leader bids me a shy goodbye and disappears into the luxurious interior of Chaiten's newest hotel. Paco insists on driving me to Casa Redonda, which actually is just a few minutes round a few corners. He promises they'll come and visit me in Las Alpujarras when they finish the race in November.

"We'll really need a holiday then!" he says laughing, filing my card into his filofax. I slide out of one world straight into another.

Chapter 24

BACK IN THE ROUND HOUSE the super-fit, adventurous Australian cyclists, Ian and Clare, look like they've lived here for ever, they're so relaxed. A few moments after I arrive, Gabor greets me curtly and then turns on Ian, who is lounging against the cooker. He lets rip with a torrent of accusations about dirty dishes being left in the sink overnight. Gabor gets into full throttle. This is our host having a paddy. Later I hear his young girlfriend has left and Andres arrived last night to play music, for hours.

The vet and the wilderness instructress are laid-back, independent travellers. They're not the slightest bit intimidated by Gabor's outpouring. And they scorn anything that smacks of an organised tour. But—having met the legend last night when he arrived with his guitar and charmed everybody—they tell me they're considering Andres's hike tomorrow.

'Vague as fog and looked-for like mail,' I think. Sylvia Plath's famous line sums up Andres for me, perfectly.

THE NEXT MORNING DAWNS BRIGHT AND SUNNY, but autumn's coming and it's getting chilly. The getaway horse is no longer waiting outside the prison; I wonder where it's gone. Clare, Ian and I head off for Andres's office. We want info about the hike the following day; Clare and Ian are still sceptical. We see the gentle Canadian—or is he really American?—talking to two travellers who have just got off the bus from Futaleufú.

Andres exudes heart-warming charm and something else, which is an extraordinary cross between mystery and brilliant, low-key salesmanship. This is, after all, his livelihood; it's how he supports his wife and two little daughters. We get involved in the conversation. I tell the newcomers about the wonderful hostal, Casa Redonda; Clare tells them about the wonderful German bakery; Andres tells them about tomorrow's hike and points them in the direction of the ferry office.

The new arrivals, Michelle, twenty eight, and Naco, about thirty four, met up in Futaleufú and spent an unforgettable day there rafting together. They're both rafting instructors and the conditions were perfect. Add a little dash of romantic sparkle and you get a very lively couple. Michelle is enchanting. They decide to stay at the Round House and to take the hike with us tomorrow. Then they disappear to book their ferry tickets. Andres turns his attention to us.

He stares at me and says "I've met you somewhere—"

"Yes," I say.

Where? He racks his memory.

"Help me," he says. Sometimes his voice becomes so quiet it's impossible to hear.

"Irish," I say—pause—

"Ahhhhhh!" he says. Then he tries the Irish greeting once again and fails.

"Ciamar a tha thu?" I say in Scottish Gaelic.

"Umm, tha gu math," he replies with a piercing smile. "Yes—Meg—I remember now."

Clare and Ian need to get on with their day. Andres notices. They require a considerable amount of information to convince them it's worth their money to take the hike tomorrow.

"We could just bike into the park and walk ourselves," they say.

"Well, no," explains Andres gently. "It's a two hour drive to get into the park before you find the trails. I'm afraid you're only allowed to walk on the designated paths, you know."

He then quietly and expertly explains the history of the Pumalín Park again. He gives a brief synopsis of the flora and fauna, including the stories of the three thousand year old trees which we saw with Marcus. He explains all about the bee farm and the exotic white blossom of the ulmo trees. He completes the picture with the dolphins on Santa Barbara beach.

"Yes," I add. "We saw about thirty dolphins last time. It was really a fabulous, unforgettable sight at sunset."

Clare and Ian are sold. There will now be five of us for the hike tomorrow, Andres says, maybe more.

"Are you coming to Casa Redonda tonight to play music?" I ask as we leave.

"I might," he replies, smiles and disappears into thin air.

MICHELLE AND NACO LOVE THE ROUND HOUSE. They stayed with Marta in Futaleufú. We swap notes over lunch. Michelle from Manchester, with her exotic transatlantic French-Canadian accent, has a charm and a love of humanity which is enchanting.

She's just finished a year teaching teenagers English in Korea. In the last few months she's explored Laos, Cambodia and Vietnam, alone. Naco's English is extraordinary. He's from northern Spain but teaches poetry in an American university. I think he's in love with Michelle, but Michelle is in love with life. Later we bump into each other leaving Casa Redonda.

"Where are you off to?" she asks brightly.

"I'm going to the cyber café," I tell her.

"I'll come too," she says, "is it far?"

"Nothing's far away in this little town!"

After checking our emails we set off to buy vegetables and wine for the supper we're planning to cook together. In a dark corner shop that looks like it's an illustration from a fifty year old children's story book, we explore the vegetable options then study the wine selection.   There's a long, wooden counter, piled high with jars, and behind there are long shelves with many empty spaces between the tins of fruit and packets of soup. The shopkeepers—three stern-looking, elderly brothers wearing white aprons—watch us unsmilingly.

In seconds, Michelle with her Peruvian hat with woolly pigtails has charmed everybody in the shop.   She asks questions in good Spanish about everything that's lying on the counter and behind. Now she's being offered samples of cheese and biscuits.

"Nice?"

"Very, very nice," Michelle replies.

The sombre mood of the shop lifts. Suddenly it's full of laughter and light.

"What's the very most delicious wine in your shop?" she asks Elder Brother. "I mean what's your absolute favourite? What would you drink for your wedding anniversary for example? Or, if you were divorced, what would you buy for your beautiful new young—wife, girlfriend?"

The three elderly brothers think this is hilarious.

"This one," replies a deep voice.

"Why?" asks Michelle, genuinely interested.

"Well—er—it's very nice—but it's—"

"Expensive? So, OK, is it going to cost me an arm and leg?"

"No, for you señorita, not expensive."

Then Michelle turns to me.

"What do you like Meg?"

"Well, when I buy wine—and I don't often—I choose it by the label. I choose the most attractive label. Look, this one's got an old fashioned bike on it—now I'd buy that just for the image!"

We buy the bike bottle and leave the brothers smiling. There's a shortage of small change in the till, so Middle Brother asks Michelle if she likes chocolate candies.

"*Si, por supuesto*," she beams—yes, of course.

Michelle is given a large handful of chocolate candies in place of our change. We leave our smiles behind and take theirs with us.

Walking slowly back to Casa Redonda we pass chickens running free and sheep tied up in front gardens. The dirt track roads in the village are wide. It's deeply shocking that just a year later, this little town will be deserted. The nearby volcano will erupt and Andres and the ten thousand inhabitants will all be evacuated by boat. As we pass the laundrette the conversation turns to our families. We exchange basic details.

"So, do you see your sons much?" Michelle asks sensitively.

"Yes, I see them about four times a year now."

"And how is it?"

This young woman always wants to know the whole truth.

"It's …well, one step forward, one step back. It gets a little easier each year that passes. You know, Michelle, it's impossible for a mother not to adore her children."

Immediately I have a flashing sense of my birth mother and my Irish grandmother and I know this statement is not completely true.

A huge sigh—an enormous longing—fills my whole being. Michelle and I continue walking, chickens scuttling beside us.

"How do you get on with your mom?" I ask my new young friend.

"Later," she says. "I'll tell you when we open the wine."

Two years later Michelle tells me her mom is the bravest person she's ever met.

In the evening Andres doesn't show up to play music. Andy and vegetarian Angela—the bookie and the lawyer—arrive, tired, from Puyuhuapi. I've made them a large pot of lentil soup which they devour hungrily and gratefully. They decide to join the hike tomorrow.

Michelle and I drink the bike-bottle wine and eat pasta. She tells me about her adventures in South Korea. Our friendship deepens. We like each other. She spreads lightness and fun wherever she goes. She's definitely being drawn by her star, everywhere. It sounds like she's a legend in Korea, already. The Universe lends me a lovely daughter for a special three days and I'm grateful.

Chapter 25

THE NEXT MORNING, we set off in the minibus. Andres gets right into his element. We'll stop for picnic supplies first, he announces. Most of us have done this already, but this is a ritual not to be omitted. This is the best bakery, he tells us. We stop. He and I linger over the wholemeal rolls together. The owners greet him with hearty pats on the shoulder and animated jokes. We pile back in the van. Then another stop. This is where you get the best German cakes he tells us. The shopkeeper greets him with a warm smile. A final stop.

"Everybody got water?"

The difference from the last hike with Marcus is total. Sunshine—not rain—touches everything living—plant, tree and creature. The autumn colours are magnificent. When we come to the first hike, where Marcus decided to be my knight in shining armour, I decide to stay behind. I'm quite tired, truth be told. My emotions have become a choppy sea. The attraction to Andres is colossal. As if zapped by a spell I didn't notice being cast, I completely forget my mission to unlock Andres's personal story and merge into an unfolding scenario which creates itself. There follows a touching and— at times—painful series of lessons in the different kinds of love available to us, which leaves me deeply opened but still ambivalent about the mystery of relationships.

How is it possible that when our hopes get raised, then dashed, we can still love the heart and soul of another unconditionally?

Like Ian, the restless cyclist, I'm feeling the need to be quiet and alone.

I tell Andres and the others I'm going to find a place to meditate; everybody knows I've done the hike before. To my surprise, Andres says he's not hiking either. We both spread out our picnic foods on a small wooden table by the roadside and then he disappears.

Our group have been given their instructions:

"Just keep bearing right all the time—never left—come back when you want; the highest waterfall is a two hour hike there and back." The same directions Marcus gave us.

I look at my lunch and then at his and can't decide what to do. We both have the same wholemeal rolls. I have a tin of tuna fish; he has a lump of cheese. I have an apple; he has a collection of chocolate biscuits. Wait or eat? I decide to eat and just as I finish and get up to look for a place to meditate, he returns.

ANDRES BEGINS TO TELL ME THE STORY of how he taught the local teenagers to make *charangos*—the instrument which looks like a cross between a banjo and a ukulele.

"Then," he says, "I taught them how to play it. Then we made a recording studio. Then we made a CD. Finally, the teenagers left school with music in their veins."

This conversation has started with a casual remark about the tone of greens that surround us in the forest. I say it would be a difficult scene for a beginner to paint because all the green tones are extreme, from almost black-green to sparkling light yellow.

"Music's like that," he says. "Every instrument has its own tone—"

And then comes the second part to the story I'd heard from Lorinda.

The charismatic explorer quietly tells me how he rescued an artist from Futaleufú who'd been victimised and persecuted by the locals. It seemed unbelievable in such a small place, but the French woman was upsetting people. She needed to leave, but didn't know where to go and had no money. Andres stepped in. He drove her three hundred and fifty kilometres to Chaiten and put her on the ferry to the island of Chiloé. She lived there with friends of his for quite a few years. It was there that her work blossomed. The next thing they heard was that she was having exhibitions in New York. I remembered Lorinda's café and the large oil painting hanging on the wooden wall.

"I have a friend called Vicky who is self-taught," I tell him. "A Canadian, like you. She's been so successful, the Queen of England even bought one of her paintings and that's just after six or seven years painting."

"Self-taught. What do you mean by self-taught?"

His tone sounds harshly critical.

His question feels loaded. I feel I've made a hugely offensive blunder. I feel in it every cell of my being.

"I mean—" I say rummaging within the depths of my truth, "—self-taught for me *usually* means the person hasn't learnt to draw. As far as I'm concerned, the only merit in a degree in art in my day, was the opportunity to draw and improve one's drawing skills every single day for four or five years. This amounts to a long apprenticeship in looking and handling drawing materials. Self-taught artists have a freedom many trained artists lose. So it's swings and roundabouts. I love drawing and for me, it's the basis of my art. In my friend's case, for example, I don't think she draws much, but she's been tremendously successful with her painting. She also knows exactly how to promote her art. I don't."

Andres listens quietly. I forget to tell him Van Gogh was also self taught—though he did take drawing lessons in 1886, for a year, at the École Nationale des Beaux-Arts in Paris.

Andres stops eating.

"I'd like to paint," he says. "But I can't."

I'm surprised by this revelation.

"Anybody can learn to paint up to a standard that will give them a lot of pleasure," I tell him. "If they find a good teacher to get them started."

"What does that mean?" he asks. "What's a good teacher?"

"Well," I say. "If you want to paint in a representational way, there are certain *basics* like composition, tone, brush techniques, colour mixing and a bit of perspective. A good teacher can teach you these things."

"I can't even mix the colours I want," he says with feeling.

"Ah, that's easy," I encourage. "I could show you how to mix twenty different greens in ten minutes."

I begin to explain about warm and cold colours. Warm colours are reds, oranges and yellows. Cold colours are blues, greens and purples. So a warm green would be a green with lots of yellow in it, a yellowy-green. A cold green would have more blue in it, a bluey-green. Scarlet has lots of yellow in it, but crimson has blue, so you can get warm reds and cool reds too.

"How do you teach composition?" he asks. "How do you know what's a good composition?"

We're both standing up now. I'm feeling very alone with him.

"I apply the golden section, always," I say. "If it's a landscape or a still life—even a portrait painting—it never fails."

Then in the dirt on the ground beside the picnic table—with the leftovers of our lunch attracting birds—I sketch with a long stick the golden section, the geometric 'formula' of perfect balance first used by the Greeks, centuries ago, later adopted by many Renaissance painters. Andres pays acute attention. The dynamic has changed between us.

I'm confident about what I'm saying, but not confident about its reception, nor where this conversation is leading. It's a strange feeling. I feel vulnerable and confused by these feelings. As I finish my 'lecture', the first of the hikers return. I'm flabbergasted to discover I've been answering his questions for nearly two hours.

I'm feeling embarrassed now. And I haven't done what I wanted to do: meditate. But I've had two hours with a man who fascinates me deeply; even though I don't think it's going very well. Andres moves towards the mini van, climbs in, takes up his ukulele/banjo and begins to play. It's bittersweet.

Half an hour later we all pile into the vehicle and head for another trail and another hike to higher waterfalls. This is the other trail Marcus and I hiked just a few weeks ago. I hang back and tell Andres I'm going to wait, I don't feel like hiking today. He climbs back into his van and continues to play the sweetest of sounds on his *charango*. I slink under a giant rhubarb plant, out of view and sink into a feeling of acute separateness.

IT'S GETTING DARK AS WE ARRIVE AT SANTA BARBARA BEACH. The colours are vibrant. The black beach is dotted with small, purple shells streaked with silver; the sky is a vast palette of melting greys and pinks, but there is no sign of the dolphins.

Andres sits in his van. He plays and sings as we spread out and walk the full length of the beach. The three couples drift off slowly. The young Croatian architect we picked up en route walks in the opposite direction. I head back for the rock where Sylvie and I sat for that unforgettable moment. It's a beautiful scene and we are all tired for different reasons. When finally we return to the van we hear Andres singing an exquisite song.

"What's it called?" Michelle asks when he finishes.

"It's called Little Ocean Rainbow," he says quietly.

"Why?" Naco asks.

"I was sailing when my daughter was born," he explains. "At the moment of her birth a rainbow spread right over our heads. So that's how she got her name."

WHEN WE RETURN TO CHAITEN, Andres wants to know who would like to make another trip tomorrow. He explains various possibilities. Everybody's catching the late night ferry tomorrow, except me and Michelle. The Croatian architect enthusiastically accepts an invitation from all of us to come and have supper with us.

"I'll bring some wine," he says.

"Bike wine's good," laughs Michelle.

Andy and Angela love hot springs, so they arrange to meet Andres at ten o'clock tomorrow morning to go with him to the springs. I'm ambivalent.

"You coming to play music tonight?" somebody asks Andres.

No reply, just a smile.

Chapter 26

THE BOOKIE AND THE LAWYER AND I wait for Andres to arrive at his office hut. It's a perfect day for a visit to the hot springs, sunny and warm. Finally, we set off with our charismatic guide oozing charm to everybody, as usual. There has been the customary late start then the usual stops for bread rolls, German cakes, water etc. Andy pushes me into the front seat, grinning. Andres starts talking to me and doesn't appear to be able to stop. He launches into a dissertation on the petrol engine versus diesel and then elaborates on the minute workings of the diesel engine.

In the next breath he tells me he's been a diver in Guatemala, that he rescued a celebrity's son there from some fate worse than death, that he and his partner were deep sea divers, that he's been a fisherman in Canada. He also talks about being a musician in Argentina in a band which became successful.

The road to the hot springs winds through more extraordinary scenery. I'm beginning to recognise different species of plants and trees now: the lofty arrayánes, the magical canelos, the calafates with their black berries, the lengas and the cipres. The white flowers of the ulmo trees look like snow from a distance. They make especially sweet honey. And the birds: eagles and condors, woodpeckers and falcons. There are pumas in the high forests, deer, foxes and armadillos somewhere, but they're hard to find.

When we arrive at the hot springs, it's a joy to find them peaceful and completely untouched by tourism. No snack bars, shops or modern changing rooms. Nothing except a couple of log cabins and three old steaming pools—one large, one medium-sized and one small—surrounded by pristine nature. I'm glad I came.

LOUNGING IN HOT SPRINGS ISN'T REALLY MY THING, so I climb out of the hottest pool after a sweltering fifteen minutes. Andy and Angela continue to bask. I see Andres walking across a track nearby, half hidden by overhanging trees. He looks at me in my blue and green bikini and I feel stranger than ever. After a short search I find a shady spot under a tall ulmo tree, beside a stream. It's a playground for hundreds of yellow butterflies and a handful of enormous, turquoise dragonflies; a perfect place to meditate. Gradually but soon, complete peace descends into every cell of my being. Time stands still. Thoughts surrender to the bigger picture which is wordless, worriless and wonderfully mysterious.

An hour later, as if by some inner telepathic alarm clock, we all drift towards Andres's van at exactly the same moment.

This beautiful man of uncertain age—forty, forty five, fifty?—our guide for just a few days in a lifetime—with shoulder-length grey, curly hair and not too broad shoulders—shifts from foot to foot. He has an unforgettably kind face and a voice that's often so quiet it's no more than a whisper. He wears the same dark blue corduroy trousers he wore the day before and the same dark blue fleece. His woolly fisherman's hat never seems to come off.

"Ready to go?" he asks.

No, not really, I think, and yet—yes, totally ready.

Once again, Andy shoves me into the front seat with a wink. It's this cheeky wink that wakes up my questioning thoughts again. What is it I really want to say to Andres? What is it I need to ask him? What is it he's been saying to me—petrol versus diesel engines—a mysterious journey all the way down from Guatemala to this one-horse town where he's become a legend, famous throughout the whole province and beyond. For what? His knowledge of the wilderness, his music—his charm—what is going on between us?—because something is, yet nothing is—if this was my film, what would happen next?

A SOFT SPACE IN MY HEART, which has been empty for three years, is making itself felt again. It's like a precarious transparent bubble. It's getting bigger by the hour, despite everything. I can picture it, feel it. But it's not safe and it's in danger of disintegrating from the slightest interference. It's also like a hard, swinging door which keeps banging shut. I know I'm mixing my metaphors here, but I don't care. This is how it is. I'm feeling bits of me I don't usually pay attention to. I'm glimpsing and wandering in and out of a vast, blissful, terrifying, uncharted inner wilderness which I think—maybe—is at the heart of all of us. When we open the heart door, we enter another world.

As we leave the van, Andres tells me he'll come round to see my paintings tonight. I'm past caring actually, I say to myself. Why am I saying this? Doors slammed shut again.

Chapter 27

"I'VE COME TO SEE YOUR ART," Andres says, without any preamble.

We've gained a new member of our shifting Casa Redonda family. Don calls himself an ancient mariner, although he's probably only about fifty five.

"I'm retired from the sea," he says. "Been all round the world many times." He's rich and lives in Karachi. His passion is fly-fishing and I overhear him telling Michelle that he's been ill recently.

"I really think it could be Mad Cow Disease," he says.

Oh hey! I think. Oh really? He's asked Gabor to give him some advice on fly-fishing. He also wants our wonderfully, colourfully, eccentric host to take him fly-fishing tomorrow. But Gabor wants to go to the hot springs with Michelle tomorrow so—it will be interesting to see what transpires.

Andres engages with Don in his usual fashion. He starts to play with words and pronunciations. Don sits at the kitchen table tying flies, wrongly it seems.

Andres asks him a question and Don replies.

"No," says Andres. "You misunderstand me."

He repeats the word. Don mispronounces it again.

"No."

This sort of ping-pong match with words goes on for longer than is comfortable. Andres seems to love this kind of banter. Will Don rise to the bait and get angry?

No—Andres at last concedes with a huge smile, but he's lost Don. Gabor appears. They greet each other casually.

Like players in a play—which we all are in so many ways—we take up our positions for the evening.

"Show me," says Andres. "Show me your paintings."

Andres looks at the art cards slowly and thoughtfully. The same ones I showed Marta and the headmaster. He lingers long over each image—the clowns, Zoshie and the Shepherd, the Persian woman with the dove, the monks, my father. Michelle sits opposite us and sees every painting upside down; it doesn't seem to matter. She feels more than just a spectator. Don continues to fiddle with flies at the table to our left. Gabor distances himself on the second step of the circular staircase which winds round the tree. He starts to play his guitar.

"I've seen the pictures before," he tells Andres.

Somehow—I don't remember how it actually happens—but the wilderness guide asks a question, to which I reply I was born in Ireland but was adopted in Scotland. But I've told him this before! Has he forgotten? Yes, of course he has. Before I know it, my adoption story—like a coiled spring—leaps right out into the open.

Andres keeps asking more questions about my childhood, my mother and my adopted parents. It's like teasing wool out of fleece; it all unfolds easily in his hands. Michelle smiles. She chips in with an occasional question or exclamation. She feels like an ally. Gabor continues to strum. Don continues to tie flies. I am aware everybody is listening. I must have decided at some point, on some level, that it's OK to tell my story. These days I feel I have a personal story, like everybody else, but I'm not my story. I'm not *consciously* acting out my dramas any more, so I can tell Andres this tale without any internal chaos going on. I believe I'm at peace with my past now—all that I can remember—and I love my new life. I have yet to have the life-changing insight about the Isla de los Muertos experience. I thought I was coming to Chile to find a story, now it seems I'm being invited to tell my own.

"THIS STORY—MY STORY—HAS A BLACK AND WHITE FEEL TO IT", I begin. "It's like an old-fashioned, X certificate, World War Two movie. It's a costume drama." Andres looks me straight in the eye. What I don't say is that it's stained with fear, betrayal and denial etched into a background of religious and superstitious Ireland. So I summarise a tale of heartbreak. I edit the story. I trust I'll know which bits to share and which bit to withhold. A psychiatrist convinced me many years ago that *'we don't have to tell anybody everything'.*

I tell Andres the setting for this 'movie' is Dublin, 1944.

The protagonists are Lionel, my father; a mysterious Jewish medical student from a privileged aristocratic background, recently fled from Europe; Lucie, my mother, a young Irish beauty newly back from London, recuperating after a minor gynaecological operation. The supporting cast—a country unable to accept illegitimacy. During the war, and after it, the Irish did terrible things to their unmarried mothers. Some situations were almost as inhuman as Auschwitz. My mother was Protestant: Jewish plus Catholic would have been much worse for both of us.

I have Andres's complete attention, so I continue. I choose my words carefully, or rather they choose themselves. In revealing a simple version of my story to him, like a film script, I later discover another story hiding inside it.

SCENE ONE.   Discovering her eldest, unmarried daughter's pregnancy, a respectable, widowed, Dublin-born woman turns into a heartless demon. She cuts up her daughters clothes so that she can't go out, locks her into the coal shed when anybody knocks on the front door, then banishes her to the north of the country to work in a hospital kitchen until the disgraceful event is over. Fallen from grace amongst her own friends after the premature death of her Dutch husband, the penniless, desperate grandmother-to-be appears to have no choice but to keep up appearances and become an—embittered—seamstress. Convinced she'll be completely damned and ostracised from Irish Society if she or her daughter has anything to do with an illegitimate child, she instructs her daughter to get rid of *"it"* as soon as *"it's"* born. There are no mitigating circumstances, however awful, that make abortions available to Irish girls. And anyway, grandmother isn't interested in my mother's story. Illegitimacy in Ireland is an unforgivable sin. It is the very worst fate that can befall any young woman. So the child must be got rid of—adopted—sent as far away as possible. End of story. But not the end of the story for me.

"You must not touch, see or feed *it* after *it's* born." Grandmother's final instructions. My mother complies.

Scene Two. Six days after my birth in Belfast, granny arrives and takes my mother to the cinema. It's a carefully selected, extremely sad film. I don't go. I've been deposited in an orphanage somewhere in Belfast.

"Cry," she says to her daughter when they sit down to watch the film. "And never, ever mention this dreadful, awful *thing* again."

The two women then return to Dublin by bus, empty-handed.

Scene Three. Six weeks later, my mother comes back to Belfast alone to collect me and take me to Scotland for adoption. We board the night boat-train; this is our first real meeting. Our one and only adventure together. This is my exile. She wraps me in a soft, white shawl she's knitted. This is the only thing she is able to give me, apart from my name. Little does my poor mother know that the kind hospital doctor who examines her baby on arrival in Edinburgh, to whom she pours out her broken heart, will be the person who adopts her child. Emma is on the lookout for a Jewish baby—although I'm not strictly speaking Jewish, as it was my father who was Jewish, not my mother.

From that point on, in the collective histories of mother, father and child, these three lives never touch each other again until forty five years later when I find my mother in Dublin. A much loved grandmother now, she refuses to tell me my father's name, or how to find him. This is without doubt the major disappointment of my life. My mother doesn't seem to understand that my exile has cost me not only the loss of my Irish family and a father, but also the loss of my Irish and Jewish heritage. But I can live with this. I've found a way.

Scene Four. Whilst I have learned to accept my loss, I think she—Lucie, poor darling—has not been able to come to terms with hers. Why else would she want to die when I turn up, aged forty five? Two years later she passes away.

THERE ARE MOMENTS when I'm telling Andres parts of this story when I think enough is enough. But Andres won't let me stop. How extraordinary, I think afterwards, here is a man who won't even tell me where he's from, wanting to know every detail of my childhood.

Much later, almost two years after this monologue, I realise it was my unsupported, widowed grandmother who was responsible for my exile from Ireland, not my mother. All my life I'd been angry with the wrong person.

Andres continues his questioning.

"What was it like when you met your real mother?" There is a pause when I wonder if I really want to impart this information.

"How was it?"

"Painful," I say. "She didn't want to be found. Part of me didn't care. I'd been furious with her all my life for giving me away. But when I met her, the other part of me longed to hear her say, *I'm so sorry this had to happen.* But sadly, none of these little words found their way out of her mouth."

"What did your adopted parents think about that, about finding her? How amazing to be adopted by two women— two doctors—they must have loved you very much?"

"No. Well they did the best they could, like we all do. We all do the best we can for our children, don't we? Their love was conditional on me being the sort of person they wanted me to be, which I wasn't and never could be. One was kind, the other wasn't. One was tall, the other small. One was wealthy, the other miserly. One was devout, the other an atheist. One believed in progressive education, the other in discipline, denial and hard work. One was English, the other Scottish! They loved to climb mountains and between them, they gave me the priceless gift of believing women can do whatever they choose in life."

After Andres has heard the story and stopped asking questions, I ask him if he'd like to choose one of the art cards to keep. He takes a long time sifting though them and narrows it down to three.

"Take them all."

"Oh I couldn't possibly," he says. "What about Michelle?"

"Yes, of course, she can choose too," I tell him. "But this is the end of my trip; I don't want to take them home."

"No," he says. "I can't take three." He accepts two. He chooses the Guatemalan girl praying and the Persian woman with the dove. I slip the third he selects—my shining father playing the violin—into the envelope while he isn't looking.

Gabor has disappeared to bed. Andres picks up his guitar. Michelle asks him to sing. Don drinks another beer.

"I'll sing you the song I composed for my daughter when she was born," he says. "We named her Little Ocean Rainbow."

We know, I say silently. We've heard it before. But we sit entranced anyway. What love this man has for his daughter. It's a poignant, almost unbearable, five minutes relieved slightly by the distracting thought that I feel I've exposed far too much of myself and there's no taking it back.

The next morning Andres returns early, unexpectedly.

"My little girls love your pictures," he tells me.

Did he come just to tell me that? He kisses me goodbye; I seem to be leaving a lot of myself here in Chaiten and a tiny little bit of myself in his home. My brain has told me to feel neutral. So I comply.

'GUATEMALAN GIRL PRAYING' PASTEL ON PAPER

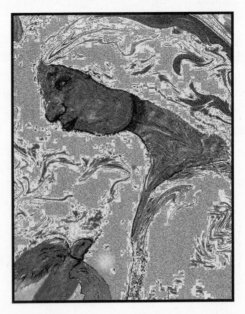

'PERSIAN WOMAN' DIGITAL IMAGE DERIVED FROM CERAMIC PLAQUE

'CLOWN' DIGITAL DRAWING

'MY FATHER' DIGITAL DRAWING

Chapter 28

'MASTER OF CEREMONIES' JUAN CARLOS, from the airport, finally arrives out of the mist to pick me up. The ancient mariner—who told Michelle he might have Mad Cow Disease—kindly phoned him on his mobile because he's an hour late and I'm beginning to think I've been forgotten.

"I'm comin'," he yells. "I'm comin'!"

He comes in the form of a large, joker of a man whose sense of humour is infectious. We joke about the misunderstanding that I wasn't on his passenger list.

"But I booked online," I'd insisted.

"No, no," he had said. "No *Meg* Robinson on the list, all the flights are booked for the next week. Sorry."

Andres stepped in and tried to help.

Finally we discovered that Robinson *Meg* is booked so—hey-ho—I can fly.

We speed off in Juan Carlos's minibus, first to his cabin office beside the German bakery, and then an hour later we roll up at the airport. Thick cloud has come down over the village, so no planes are getting in or out of Chaiten. After a wait of another three hours, a tiny plane arrives. It's a four-seater Cessna from Chiloé Island. Three Americans without luggage run out and squeeze into it.

Finally our plane arrives and eight of us climb aboard. The other passengers are all locals. Flying high above the Andes, we look down on the myriad of tiny islands and fascinating fingery fjords we would have seen close to, had the ferry become an option.

Landing at Puerto Montt is easy and smooth, then suddenly I realise the minibus we've transferred to is hurtling away from the airport. I need to catch another flight at the same airport. When the confusion is sorted I'm returned to the departure lounge for a five hour wait.

PUERTO MONTT AIRPORT IS BUSY. Outside, the cloud has slunk down again; it's thick and grey. I particularly notice a few passengers during what turns out to be a seven hour wait. I watch them like instalments of a soap opera. There's an older man with a weather-beaten, wrinkled face carrying a brown, leather briefcase. He's wearing an eye-catching yellow anorak and seems to be unable to sit down. There's a young Chilean couple whose two adventurous, crawling babies tirelessly explore every inch of the departure lounge. A group of sophisticated Brazilian tourists—three men and a tall woman—all wearing gold watches, sport expensive winter overcoats draped over their shoulders. They drink endless cups of coffee and check the time repeatedly.

At half past seven in the evening we get called to the departure lounge. I should have realised something is wrong when there is no security check whatsoever.

We sit and wait. It's now nine thirty.

The other airline flight to Santiago is called and I watch as the latecomers get later and later. How can anybody arrive for a flight half an hour after its departure time? Yet more and more people still trickle through. Then somebody spreads the story the airport is closing and our flight is cancelled till tomorrow.

There follows chaos, Chilean style.

The men and I head for the check-in desk in a posse, the women disappear. No more flights tonight, we're told, come back tomorrow. Some of the men get angry. I just observe. There are only two flights tomorrow. Anybody can work out that they can't get another sixty people onto two full planes. So what's going to happen? I wonder whether to rebook with the expensive airline company. Two businessmen seem to be doing this. I decide to go with the main flow and return tomorrow with the crowd.

The men go home. An hour later the airport is practically empty. After an incredibly long time trying to get a phone to work, a hotel to give me a room, a shuttle bus to return and pick me up, I finally leave the airport at a quarter to eleven with the fatherly airport manager making sure the shuttle bus has arrived for me. I'm heading for a hotel in the somewhat risky harbour area of Puerto Montt, described in the guidebook as modern! Funny, though, how jewels turn up in the most unexpected places.

MY ROOM WILL BE ON THE FOURTH FLOOR of the recommended modern hotel. When I explain I'm the person who's just phoned from the airport, the receptionist starts laughing and doesn't appear to be able to stop. She takes a good long look at me then takes an equally long time choosing a room key. I'm not sure what the joke is! Is this a brothel? She hands me my key, still sniggering.

The hotel is a labyrinth of long empty narrow red carpeted corridors. We're close to the railway station and the busy harbour. The area reminds me of San Francisco's Mission district, but smaller. It's scary.

Exiting the four-person lift, the fourth floor seems to be quiet. My room is smallish, with two beds and a miniature bathroom. It feels warm and clean.

There are traffic lights just below the window and every time cars stop, two young street performers jump into action. One brandishes—then throws—two flaming torches high into the black night sky. The other drums loudly. Their act is perfectly timed. They know exactly how long they've got before the lights change. Four or five flaming thrusts into the inky sky, then a quick sprint along the cars to collect money. It's a short, exhilarating show but soul-destroying, because nobody at this time of night gives them any money. I'm overwhelmed with empathy for them. I want to go down and be generous, much more generous than I was with the angel in the tunnel—but something stops me. I resist. A firm inner voice cautions me:

"Not a good idea Meg, it's almost midnight, very dangerous; think where you are." Yes, you're right. Maybe they'll be back in the morning. The young entertainers get less energetic each time the lights change. Now they're gone. Silence. Day over. I wonder how much they made today. Who will they go home to? Where will home be?

I'm extremely thankful to have a bed for the night but I'm still not one hundred per cent sure I'm in a safe place. After a hot shower, I switch on the wall-mounted television. It's late now, about eleven thirty, the day before Good Friday. A Russian choir is performing somewhere in Chile. Suddenly, exquisite voices fill my bedroom.

The music is modern, exciting, original, profoundly moving and extremely avant-garde. It becomes wildly beautiful and then sublime. I feel that familiar excitement again; my imagination has been torched. It's like thirty angels are reminding me I'm *always* being drawn by a star.

Even when I forget, beauty and peace are still everywhere, in the spaces between words and thoughts, in the seedy street outside, in this room, in this hotel which may or may not be a brothel.

I'm glowing inside. I wedge the chair in front of the door, lie down on my narrow bed and surrender to bliss. Everything that's happened today suddenly dissolves into sound: Andres's farewell kiss, Juan Carlos and the long wait for the tiny plane, flying over the awesome Andes, the chaos and the anger at the airport, the pantomime to get a place to stay. My bedroom becomes a sacred space. The performance is unforgettable. Sometimes the choir, dressed in purple gowns, stop singing and just whisper in three parts. It's exquisite; it's extraordinary.

I'm very tired. The day started with a sweet goodbye from the man who captured my heart and is ending with sublime music and street theatre. Am I OK? Am I safe? Am I being looked after? Have I found my story? Have I found my tribe? Is there more to come? What about the crisis? The music zaps this last thought instantly.

I think I'll take a holiday now. I knew I wouldn't rest until I'd accomplished my mission. One week left in Chile, time to be a different kind of explorer, a city explorer. I think I'll head for Valparaiso on the coast and explore the colourful world of the poet Pablo Neruda, whose home there is now a museum.

The Russian singers continue to thrill and bathe every cell in my being. I'm being cleaned on the inside, recharged, refreshed and reminded about the power of music, the magic of creativity, and the inspiration of Divine love. It's almost Easter and the choir are singing and whispering love songs about a gentle man who died a very long time ago in horrendous circumstances.

My film will have sublime music. Their music? I scrabble to find a pen to write down the name of the choir, but fall asleep, biro in hand, before the programme ends.

> *"What keeps us alive, what allows us to endure?*
> *I think it is the hope of loving,*
> *or being loved."*
> *(Master Eckhart)*

And then ... the crisis, the insights and the screenplay

THE LONG-AWAITED CRISIS HAPPENS three days after I return to Spain, the morning after the clown and the actress come to supper. A neighbour has been watering my indoor plants and considering me a hopeless gardener; she's moved them to sunnier places around the house. I start to rearrange them. Not noticing the trail of water they're leaving, I slip on the unforgiving terracotta tiles and shoot forward onto my face. My hands and toes act as brakes. Many little bones in my right foot get smashed and the left big toe cracks like a dropped hard-boiled egg. The palms of my hands turn purple. I pull myself into bed and stay there for 24 hours.

The Insights

'It always seems impossible until it's done.'
(Nelson Mandela)

WITH THE PASSING OF TWO YEARS and the travel memoir almost completed, insights started to tumble in. I've come to realise that Tortel was the real crisis. Anton the tarot reader was right.

"You will learn something very valuable through the crisis," he said. And I have. Through writing about it, the bigger picture, the purpose of the journey, has gradually emerged. Then the insights brought their gifts. And the learning continues and continues and never seems to stop.

I started this book by saying that my personal stories these days are mostly defused; they don't carry pain. One story, however—unknown to my conscious mind—has been hibernating in the basement of my heart, charged with enormous pain and in the middle of the printing process of this book, it's leapt to life and begged to be healed. Its voice simply would not let me walk away.

BUT BACKTRACKING SLIGHTLY. TWO YEARS AFTER completing the story part of this book, somebody asked me 'What have you learnt from this adventure? People will want to know.' Thinking about this, the insights began arrive.

I've come to see that many of my 'lessons' in Patagonia are also the life lessons of countless other people all around the world. Many of us have a primal wound or wounds— abandonment, shame, unworthiness— that, when touched, call, whisper, moan, groan or rage to be healed. This is the story within the story that I've discovered. After my return from Chile, in sharing parts of my own story of losing my daughter, I've discovered that what is most personal in our wounds is most universal.

After that unforgettable evening on the black volcanic beach watching families of dolphins playing in the grey blue water, just after sunset, when Sylvie came and sat beside me, when my sadness and secrecy surrounding the termination of my daughter Katie's life was momentarily triggered, it has been the secrecy issue that has come back to haunt and torture me. I have agonised about including it in this book. After much soul searching, prayer and meditation, I've decided to include it, because finally, the truth of it has set me free. After 36 years of keeping a large part of myself hostage, I'm giving up on shame. In this unlocking, liberating, letting-go process, I've come to experience that we are never, ever the only person who feels that their life has been irreparably scarred or damaged or blighted by shame. This is the most valuable lesson I have learnt by being drawn by my star to Patagonia.

With awareness and acceptance of what has been and a belief in a loving Higher Power, or the bigger picture—call God what you like, The Universe, Great Spirit, Allah—my experience is that peace replaces disgrace, unimaginable damage can be healed and our scars make us beautiful—*'It always seems impossible until it's done'* as Nelson Mandela has said.

An extraordinarily courageous Irish man in Dublin whose daughter disappeared thirty years ago (and who has never been found) said to me after I was invited to tell my adoption story on a late night Irish TV chat show in the year 2000,

"Our scars make us beautiful, Meg."

I believed him—and then forgot.

This conviction is one of the main themes of the film.

Isla de los Muertos

THE SENSING OF BLISS with a partner in a previous life on the Isla de los Muertos took me by complete surprise. Many people call this experience *soul retrieval*. This may well be the real reason I was drawn so strongly to Tortel in the first place. I glimpsed an immense happiness on the island that I haven't experienced in this lifetime with either husband, not by any means their entire fault.

As a result of this insight, the next shocking realisation has been that I've drowned my belief in partnership, in intimate personal happiness, following the death of my daughter. I've been paying the price for my sadness and my one million private-to-the-grave *what-ifs* ever since, with a few brief respites. And my 'shut down' has gravely harmed a few significant others along the way.

Quickly following these painful realisations, with the help of a wise friend, a new compassionate belief has taken root in my whole being.

Challenges of adoption

Many adoptees, abandoned and long-term abducted children and children who were not wanted by their parents have specific, difficult, life challenges and deeply unconscious fears to deal with, as do bereaved parents. I'm seeing now that I haven't drowned my belief in togetherness with family, lovers and friends; I haven't *sabotaged* my own happiness. Rather, I've hidden it to protect it from further hurt. If I choose to, I can find where I've buried it, dig it up and start living life differently, openly, without any secrecy. I understand that this will take time and practice to master.

As adults, many, but not all adopted or unwanted children find love deeply confusing. Those of us who do, do the best we can, and—I think—we can do better if we so choose. This is what I've learnt. It's not a case simply of 'getting over it'—the abandonment—because what's been missing is unknown—mother love. We can't describe the pain of the void. The agony of not being wanted. Of not fitting in. But the way forward seems to be a case of accepting this and seeing ourselves simply as individual people in the world with unique gifts to share.

Babies and children exiled from Ireland because of their illegitimacy were once a group deeply scorned—not wanted. Many, mainly Catholics, who were permitted to stay in their country, were locked up in institutions, without reprieve. None of us knew what it was to be cherished by our Irish families. Now, if we choose to, we can be trail-makers for compassion and creativity. As Rachel and Jerome will be in the film.

And finally ...

THE MAGNETIC PULL TO ANDRES, ending in telling him my adoption story, seems to have been—amongst many other things—a key to discovering that I've been angry with the wrong person all my life.

Then, at the eleventh hour, when the book is ready to be sent off to be printed, another astonishing insight arrives! Thanks to a book by American Brandon Bays, like a sharp slap in the face, an intuitive thought suddenly finds its mark. Could my Irish grandmother also have lost a baby in heartbreaking circumstances? Is this why she turned into a monster? Has history repeated itself three times? Is her story a 1920's costume drama; same themes as her daughter—fear, betrayal, denial, secrecy, etched into the background of religious and superstitious Ireland?

Like a laser beam, this thought pierces the very depths of my being and considering this scenario, my heart instantly and completely collapses into a sea of compassion for my poor, beautiful, Irish mother and my suffering, Celtic, monster grandmother. The truth will never be known, but the story now *feels* understandable, complete and finished. A family drama ended. No more unwanted babies.

Film Synopsis
Drawn by a Star

WEALTHY (but soon to be disinherited) talented artist/
dancer Rachel's illegitimate infant daughter is abducted in
Paris. She meets Bolivian musician Jerome, ex-junkie street-
kid, now teacher and performer of circus arts, who helps
her scour Paris for the baby. A psychic convinces them that
they will not find the child, but she will find them when she's
eighteen, in South America.

They emigrate to Bolivia, funded by the sale of a small
stolen icon painting belonging to Rachel's father, and
begin a new life teaching hundreds of street children dance
and circus skills. Their street theatre company attracts
government acclaim and they're invited to tour Europe
with the show. Three years later during a political rally
in La Paz, heartbreak hits again. Their two year old son
dies when a stampeding crowd surges and falls on top of
Jerome. Distraught Jerome resorts to his old drug habit and
soon finds himself in prison. Rachel falls into a bottomless
depression. After a chance encounter with an inspirational
prison visitor, an old clown from Chile, Jerome decides to
leave Bolivia when he's released. The couple head by bus for
Tortel in Patagonia. Jerome becomes a fisherman. Rachel
swings in and out of severe depression loosing herself in her
art and dance. She creates exquisite installations in nature,

shelters and simple driftwood sculptures, totem poles and shrines to her lost children. She dances at night on desolate beaches. Jerome often witnesses this and from his boat, he becomes her archetypal guardian playing melodies on his charango that pacify her moods.

Slowly and gradually, fascinated by Rachel's art and Jerome's music, the local people, a collection of fiercely independent pioneers, befriend them. A year later, following a dramatic fall from a ladder, Rachel suffers a miscarriage. Their relationship collapses. Chaos and despair follow. Rachel leaves Tortel for a nearby island (Isla de los Muertos) planning her own death by eating poisonous berries. During the gathering and eating of the berries she's visited by the spirits of the island. They arrive in tiny boats filled with nightlights. Disembarking singing, they lead her to rest in a beautiful sanctuary, a small domed shelter made of branches and leaves. Inside the floor is covered with rose petals. She's found there two days later by Jerome, unconscious but alive. As a result of this experience, Rachel begins to see and experience the bigger spiritual picture of her life.

Ten years on, the couple live in a large wooden cabin owned by the grandfatherly Abraham. Surrounded by eucalyptus trees, they live beside a turquoise lake. They've taught their four little boys circus skills.

The whole family earn a living by performing street theatre to tour buses that regularly stop to view the lake where two colours meet but don't mix. Abraham plays the accordion.

The film ends with Rachel's elderly alcoholic mother Annabel arriving by bus from France with eighteen year old Sasha, the abducted baby, now a music student, a singer. Compassion and forgiveness are only possible with the 'creative' support of Jerome, Abraham and the four little boys, when it's discovered Rachel's wealthy late father arranged the abduction.

CAN I DO THIS? Can I make these characters come alive? Can I translate these images and ideas into a film? Can I explain the 'back story'? It seems a colossal undertaking. I recall the meeting with my sculptor friend beside the lottery kiosk on the first day of January last year and I remember *knowing* in my bones that this is going to happen.

"Hope is the thing with feathers that perches in the soul, and sings a tune without words and never stops at all."
(Emily Dickinson)

Author's note

THE WORDS of the late, much loved, Irish writer John O'Donohue resonate deeply with me.

"It is strange," he says, *"being here. The mystery never leaves you alone."*

If you are reading this note before reading my book, I say this to you. Thank you for considering reading it. It's a little more than a travel memoir. In 2007 my inherited Celtic love of storytelling drew me to Patagonia in search of a story to make into a film. I was drawn by 'my star'. I found my film story and then found bits of my own inner story, my own personal myth, hidden beneath it all. Voicing all these stories—from many levels—has been an exciting journey which has lasted two years. There have been three drafts to the book, three different versions. Each new draft resulted from a question somebody asked. The last being 'what have you learnt from your journey to Patagonia?' In this soul-searching I discovered many surprising things, the main being a belief that we are the sum total of all our ancestors. I believe we are here because they dreamed the best for their own lives; their dreams and short-comings are in our blood. Using creativity as a tool, with new understanding, compassion and acceptance we can make sure no further lineage of depression, fear, disappointment, hatred, judgement or secrecy need be passed onto the next generation. This is what I have learnt. The film story is an inspirational, archetypal hero's journey. An art-filled,

South American adventure to find acceptance, forgiveness, compassion, openness and joy after unimaginable loss.

And a footnote for those who have just read the book.

Since writing this book, I've visited Peru and a new chapter in my life has opened up.

Initially, I wrote this book just to remember all the adventures I'd had in Patagonia; the second draft was to be for my grandchildren. Finally, I realised the depth and wisdom of Catherine Ann Jones advice to writers:

"Your job as an author is to find the story within the story. The healing transformation of good writing depends on making it your own from within. In other words, what you write is not separate from your deepest self. These are the stories needed today. First you must discover meaning for yourself in the story. Then discover the necessary form that can make it meaningful to others."

I hope I've managed to do this. All the insights tumbled in at the end, two years after the journey ended. I kept thinking I'd finished the book and then up would pop yet another little piece of the inner jigsaw. But this one has to be the last.

Returning via Dublin from visiting my baby grand-daughters, sitting on a plane full of lively Irish holiday makers heading for sunny Spain, my eye catches this headline on somebody's Irish Times newspaper. Synchronicity kicks in. I weep on and off for the next two weeks with a sense of completion. At long last, my exile is being publicly, nationally acknowledged. Along with thousands of others who were not permitted to stay in their own Irish homes or homeland, I receive the apology I never, ever dreamed possible. The article reads:

29/07/09 People of Ireland desperately sorry.

The Irish president Mary McAleese declares publicly:

"The people of Ireland are desperately sorry for the many ways in which you were not cherished, in the abuse (from the system), in the silence, in the failure to act, in the failure to listen, hear and believe in time. I offer everyone whose little lives were robbed of the joys of childhood our heartfelt sorrow. What's learnt in childhood is engraved in stone. You met bad engravers; the children of today and tomorrow rely on us to engrave well."

Acknowledgements

MY DEEPEST GRATITUDE goes to the following people for their love, inspiration and encouragement in my life.

Multi-media artist Rachel Mackie for sharing my excitement in all my creative endeavours and for being the best email buddy in the world. Musician Helen Mallen for her bravery, her gifts of appreciation and true friendship since we were five and six years old. Elaine Cummins, my kind, brave and compassionate 'chosen' older sister. My inspirational artist friends Vicky Lentz in Canada, Naomi Mindlezum, Jana and Mark Tuschmann in San Francisco. My lost soul-friend, driftwood-sculptor Matthew F, for three unforgettable fun-filled, magical years. Two mentors, French Didier Danthois (a clown and spiritual teacher) and Austrian Gernot Dick (artist-photographer-wilderness guide), who showed me other ways of being and new ways of expressing myself in my paintings and in my life. Ram Dass and Andrew Harvey for their teachings, which led me through the desert of disbelief to find a direct path to the Divine. Father Abbot and Brother Finnbar at Pluscarden Abbey in Scotland for their wise, laughter-filled spiritual guidance and inspiration. Christian Bollman, for his beautiful music and extraordinary Watsu healing. Artist Ainsley Pratt my computer graphics teacher, for years of ever-patient encouragement. Catherine Ann Jones for her inspiring writing advice. To the wonderful Spanish people of the village where I live, for their love and for allowing me to be part of them. To Mama Sharon, a brand new mentor and inspiration for my unfolding work in Peru. Brandon Bays for her journey to find my Irish grandmother. Maggie Whiteley for her proof read and her God-given gift for illuminating the bigger picture. Katie Griffiths for her painstaking first edit and Jeni Lupton for her truly marathon final edits. And finally to dear Fay Fullerton, the kindest of friends during the most challenging early years.

This book would never have been written, and my life might easily have collapsed into nothingness, had it not been for the unconditional love and healing I received from James Baldwin and Matthew Kayser, two young healers in Scotland, fourteen years ago. I owe everything that is lovely in my life today to them. They helped me find the new me and after all the traumas, my life thereafter could only ever be one little miracle after another.

Special thanks to Janak Jani for his Footprints guidebook, without which I would not have found Tortel, nor Rachel or Jerome, or this story.

And thank you God for Andres. May his little daughters bring him oceans of joy.

TWO WEEKS BEFORE sending this manuscript to be printed, I meet Jonathan, a medium and a teacher at the London College of Psychic Studies. He deserves a very special thank you. He gives me a priceless gift, a message from my Jewish grandmother who died in a concentration camp. He tells me my grandmother wants me understand that it's time to come out of my exile now, it's time to share what I've learnt with the world. It's time to dance with everybody in the village she says; how extraordinary I think, it's the village fiesta next weekend. He tells me she died in a burst of light, her faith having been an inspiration to thousands in the camp, and in her life. She tells me I was healer in a village in a previous life. Start exploring relationships again, gently, she says through Jonathan, talk to the people you sit beside, everywhere. This extraordinary young man recounts many more things she wants me to know, but they are private. I am still a little secretive.

THANK YOU for sharing my journey. May your own journey be truly wonderfully blessed.

The film is dedicated to the memory of Jenny Mallen (31) to Carmen Cummins (3) and to the disappeared Madeleine McCann. And to all parents who have lost a child, and to all children who have lost their parents.

A note on the proceeds of this book

Eighty per cent of the proceeds from the sale of this book will go to www.pathoftheheart.org – Dr Sharon Forrest's charity which supports street children in Peru – and to www.highmountainaidperu.com – an aid project set up by Wither Avellaneda and Meg Robinson. This project brings winter supplies to seventy high mountain indigenous families near Machu Picchu.

Photographs and Paintings

A Companion book of photos of Patagonia, and Meg Robinson's paintings, **Adventures in Patagonia** is available though www.blurb.com. Proceeds to the Peru Charities

Feedback

Feedback regarding the book and donations to the two Peruvian charities will be welcomed through the website: www.healingartjourneys.com

17562464R00170

Printed in Great Britain
by Amazon